# To Hear the

## A Memoir of Aberfan

Huw Lewis was born in Merthyr Tydfil in 1964 and raised in Aberfan. He studied chemistry at Edinburgh University from which he returned to teach at Afon Taf High School, Troed-y-rhiw, before being elected to the Welsh Assembly in 1999. He represented Merthyr Tydfil and Rhymney from 1999 until 2016 holding several posts in government including the role of Minister for Education and Skills. He lives in south Wales with his wife, Lynne, and his sons James and Sam.

# To Hear the Skylark's Song

## A Memoir of Aberfan

Huw Lewis

PARTHIAN

Parthian, Cardigan SA43 1ED
www.parthianbooks.com
First published in 2017

ISBN 978-1-912109-72-2
Cover design by The Undercard
Cover image: Cottrell Street, Aberfan 1964 by James Kessell. Courtesy of Zion Methodist Chapel, Aberfan.
Edited by Dai Smith
Typeset by Elaine Sharples
Printed and bound by Pulsio
Published with the financial support of the Welsh Books Council
The Modern Wales series receives support from the Rhys Davies Trust
A cataloguing record for this book is available from the British Library.

Dedicated to the families of Aberfan and Merthyr Vale

## *Historical Note*

One hundred and forty-four people were killed in the Aberfan disaster. One hundred and sixteen of them were children. Pantglas Junior School took the full force of the landslide of slurry that surged down the mountainside at high speed when a colliery waste tip, Pantglas Tip No.7, became destabilised by a combination of heavy rain and the action of mountain springs beneath the tip. That day, Friday 21st October 1966, was the last school day before the half-term holiday. The children had been in school only a few minutes when it happened.

On Wednesday 28th October 1966, a mass funeral for eighty-one of the child victims of the disaster was held at Aberfan cemetery. The work of recovering bodies from the wreckage of Pantglas School and the houses of Moy Road, which was still progressing, was temporarily halted for the duration of the service. Two long trenches were cut into the steep hillside to serve as mass graves. Thousands of relatives and friends attended. Thousands more from other Valleys' communities came to show their respect and sympathy. They stood on the slopes of Merthyr Vale mountain across the valley, opposite the cemetery and from where they could see the form of a vast cross, made up of hundreds of wreaths, laid out on the ground next to the graves. The service was short and simple. Two hymns, some prayers, and it was done.

The South Wales coalfield had seen many mining disasters over a century or so of mining, but Aberfan was different. It was different most importantly because the victims had not been miners working underground, but children in the supposed safety of their school, as well as people in their own homes. Aberfan was also different because its suffering was witnessed by the world through television reports. The impact of the reporting on the public consciousness, not only across the UK, but around the world, could not have been greater. Like the volunteer rescue workers who had travelled to Aberfan to help, thousands of others felt the need to 'do something', and so many began to donate money. Contributions to the Aberfan Disaster Fund flooded in from all over the globe. By the time it was closed to further donations, there was around £1.7 million in the fund, more than £20 million in today's money. Some of the money was used for the relief of survivors and the bereaved, for the repair of houses, and for the building of memorials at the Pantglas school site and Aberfan Cemetery.

The people of Aberfan and Merthyr Vale demanded the removal not just of the slurry that had cascaded into the village, but of all the remaining tips that still loomed over the two villages. Neither the government nor the National Coal Board wanted to pay for it. Although the government did eventually grant £200,000 to the NCB to start the work, it also, disgracefully, dipped into the publicly donated Disaster Fund, taking £150,000 from it. In essence the people of Aberfan themselves ended up paying a large part of the cost of the clear-up operation that followed the disaster that had taken the lives of so many of their loved ones.

On 26th October 1966, the Secretary of State for Wales appointed a tribunal to establish the causes of the disaster. Within about eleven weeks the tribunal concluded that the blame for what had happened rested with the National Coal

Board, describing their actions as '...a terrifying tale of bungling ineptitude'. The NCB eventually paid out compensation at a rate of £500 per child victim, plus some money for traumatised survivors.

These are the recorded events that happened in the aftermath of the Aberfan disaster. They encompass both outpourings of sympathy and fellow feeling on the part of the public, and a bewildering callousness on the part of the NCB and the government. These are the recorded facts. But the living truth of the aftermath of that October day was that the village had to somehow carry on being and living, for all the days to come. That was not something that could be put aside by the conclusions of an inquiry, or eased with any form of compensation. At the heart of that truth was the burden of loss. Of grief. And for some, including some survivors, a psychological burden of guilt, undeserved but nevertheless real. There was trauma too for some of the rescue workers; trauma that would never leave them.

How does one live with the loss of a child? Only those who have suffered such a wrong can ever know the answer. Seneca, the Roman stoic philosopher, once said: 'Sometimes even to live is an act of courage'. I grew up surrounded by people who displayed that kind of courage every day. They still do.

# *A Note on Memory*

Memories are fragile things. Much more often than not, they are shattered into pieces by the relentless action of time. So we can only try, when time has moved on, to arrange these broken pieces, this kaleidoscope of fragments, into some kind of picture that makes sense to us. Many of the fragments are brightly coloured, vivid even, in their brightness. No doubt that is why they have survived time so well. But the relationship between each of these fragments poses a problem when we come to tell the tale of our past. This is not just a problem concerning the correct sequence of events; it is also a problem of emphasis, of inclusion and omission.

Many people will have memories of Aberfan in the times that I describe in this book, and they too will have their collection of fragments of memory. Almost always they will differ from mine and they will differ one to another, since each person's collection of fragments is unique.

Some will have memories that are clear and bright and, as such, important to them, but ones that I do not share and cannot truthfully relate in these pages. Some may have memories that conflict in some way with those I have written here. If so, please believe that although all the memories set down here are partial, imperfect, even damaged, they are even so, true to me. I have rendered them as faithfully as I am able, making no claim of any kind to any monopoly of truth.

I was very young at the time of the disaster itself; much too young to fully comprehend the enormity of what had happened. Slowly, as I grew, individual details of the story of that day and of the immediate aftermath emerged bit by bit in conversation with family and friends. Some aspects of the story

– my father's experience, for example – were only revealed to me decades after the event. Despite all this I think it right, even necessary, to write down these, my memories. In these pages I try my best to relate just what it was like to grow up in Aberfan amidst the aftershocks of trauma, and the challenges faced by a grieving community. What is most apparent to me now, is that despite the unique and devastating experience of that community, my childhood (and I think the childhood of many of us that were too young to be directly hurt by the events of that day in 1966) was happy, secure and in almost every aspect, ordinary. I did not know at the time that many of the people of Aberfan and Merthyr Vale worked hard to ensure that was the case.

I am not a survivor of Aberfan, nor am I one of the bereaved. I would not ever presume to speak for them, or pretend that I understood what they have endured. I write here simply in an attempt to relate what kind of place that village was, afterwards, and what kind of childhood it offered me. Despite everything, it was a warm and wonderful place to grow up in. I look back now with a deep affection for that Aberfan of the 1960s and '70s, and with a deep admiration too.

If a story is not told, then it is forgotten. The story of Aberfan should not be forgotten. It is simply too significant. When my generation passes, the disaster of October, 1966 and the stories of its aftermath will fade from living memory. Then our children will rely on the written word, on photographs and recorded voices, in order to make sense of what happened. This is my contribution. I know there will be others. All are important.

# Prologue

## Aberfan, 21st October 1966

This is my earliest memory. I am just shy of three years old. My sister Allyson, aged seven, leaves for school as usual that morning, but she is back again within a half hour. She tells our mother that her best friend is dead. This is all she says, or will ever say, about that day.

The black water pursues her down the hill from Pantglas School. It is at her heels the whole way. Our street – Cottrell Street – is the lowest-lying in the village, on the floor of the valley and near to the river, so the black water flows downhill toward us, undercutting a thick morning mist.

I do not know it yet but this is the water that has lifted up a man-made mountain of colliery waste and has turned that waste to slurry, so that gravity does the rest.

Peering through the open front door from behind my mother's skirts, I see it coming. Little enough at first, it trickles along the gutter like blackest ink, down the slope of Wingfield Street and across the road towards us in a burgeoning flow. It begins by sounding playful, like a stream. Then becomes forceful and strong, like a river's rush. It has the acrid and familiar smell of wet coal dust. Soon it overflows the gutters and begins to cover the pavements and the road. When three or four inches deep, it hits the front walls of the terrace and turns at right angles, roiling and protesting at the forced change of direction. It never quite makes it over our front step, but it flows fast and steady down the street all that morning, swirling and lustrous black.

I am too young to understand exactly what is going on. I have no exact knowledge of what has happened to Pantglas School or the children within it. I do not know that during the course of that morning, part of Pantglas Tip No.7, made up of thousands of tons of coal slurry, has detached and slid down the mountainside, hitting the school at high speed. I do not know that one hundred and forty-four people would die that morning, just a few hundred yards from our house, and that one hundred and sixteen of them would be children.

But it is true that we all understand more than we could ever put into words; children most of all. I know that the world has been rearranged. Shifted. What was solid ground is now liquid. The warmth and safety of our home is now tainted with the threat of impermanence. I know that somehow the world beyond our front door is suddenly threatening. I feel this rather than think it. I feel it as a knot in the pit of my belly.

Mam watches the water with bewilderment and anxiety on her face. She fears it will overtop the step and make it into the house. Sometime later that morning my Dad appears on the pavement opposite our front door, where the black water is shallowest. Inexplicably, he is home from work in the middle of the morning, still wearing his jacket and tie.

My mother and father speak together, half shouting across the road. Mam sits me on the third step of our stairs and gives me my baby brother to hold. He is heavy with sleep and still warm from his cot. He is wearing baby pyjamas with feet, not like my grown up ones. It is normally impossible to hold onto baby Gareth; usually he is in constant motion, wriggling and squirming 'like a maggot' as my Nana would say. Not this morning, though. He sits still with me, staring as the liquid coal rushes by the open door smelling, as I do, its wet, sulphurous stench.

The baby thus installed, Mam heads for the cupboard under the stairs and re-emerges with the garden spade and Dad's fishing boots. Then, one by one, she hurls each item over the road to him with an urgent strength that I hadn't known she possessed until this moment. Across the street Dad puts on his boots and throws back his work shoes underhand. They clatter into the front passage. Then he picks up the spade and is gone. I will not see him again for some days.

When finally, the front door is closed, we retreat to the middle room and the dry heat of the coal fire. I realise suddenly that I am cold. The black water has lapped the doorway of our home but it has not entered. Not quite. The slurry has not reached us either. Allyson is safe at home. We are lucky.

I stare through the window over to Merthyr Vale mountain and watch pulses of fine grey drizzle drift up the valley, like great long winding sheets of gauze, towering above us all. Slowly they knot themselves together, then drift apart, then come together once again, repeating this over and over; a churning anxiety patterned in the sky.

# Home

The Taff Valley narrows as the river runs down from Merthyr. By the time the river has flowed five miles, and reached the sibling villages of Aberfan and Merthyr Vale, the valley floor can be crossed in a five-minute walk, and the mountain sides rise steep on either side. The closeness of each mountain narrows the sky and restricts any direct sunlight that might reach the villages; the shadow of one mountain delaying the dawn, and the shadow of the other hastening the sunset.

Today this valley is verdant and looks unspoiled, even though in reality barely a square foot of it has not been turned over, tunnelled into or had coal waste heaped upon it. It is a man-made landscape, softened now by nature. In my childhood this landscape looked different. It smelled different. It even sounded different.

Like all the valleys in this part of the South Wales coalfield, the Taff Valley runs roughly north to south. It is capped in the north by the town of Merthyr Tydfil and terminates in the south with the village of Quakers Yard; barely more than a dozen miles from top to bottom. The lie of the land has always dictated the shape of anything that man has wanted to build here, and the villages of Aberfan and Merthyr Vale are no exception. When the Merthyr Vale Colliery was first sunk in 1869, the Victorian engineers were forced to divert the river in order to reclaim enough level ground to establish a pit head. In those days a colliery of that sort of scale might employ more than two thousand men, and there was an urgent need to provide housing for the new workforce and their families. Houses were thrown up quickly, in the cheapest and easiest way possible. This is why the two villages have the 'linear' shape so common in South Wales, with long terraces of houses following the contours of the ground, spooling out from the pit, and aligned roughly north to south. Those streets that connect them, running east to west, tend to be short and on a steep – sometimes very steep – gradient.

The housing was cheaply made and of poor quality. With the exception of some larger homes used by the families of managers (or perhaps the clergy) they sit, in general, on shallow foundations. Some were even built with proper brickwork or stonework featuring only at the front of the building, the rear walls being literally 'thrown together' by pouring a mixture of concrete and rubble between wooden boards.

These pit villages are not places like the towns of Breconshire to the north, or those of the Vale of Glamorgan to the south, settlements which evolved by slow accretion over many generations, all with their ancient place names and Norman churches, their local squirearchies and a mention in the Domesday Book. These pit villages were places that emerged fully formed, like mushrooms, almost overnight (indeed, there is a part of Merthyr colloquially referred to, to this day, as 'Mushroom Town' for this very reason). Houses, pubs, churches and chapels were all planned in from the very start, and all of them paid rent to the mine owner. Constructed in haste and on the shallowest of foundations, these were places always on the edge of anyone's consideration, save for those who lived here.

The two new villages drew new people, sometimes from elsewhere in the coalfield, since some experienced miners would be needed, but also from further afield. People came to Aberfan and Merthyr Vale from all over rural Wales, from the west of England, from Ireland and even Spain and Italy. Both my mother and my father were born in Merthyr Vale, but into families of such incomers. The Pierces, my mother's family, had their roots in the slate quarrying communities of north Wales. The Lewises, on my father's side, had mixed Welsh and Irish heritage.

Iron was still produced in Merthyr in those early days, and coal and iron together formed the economic base for everything that happened in the valley. Connected first by canal and then by rail with the ports of Cardiff and Barry so that these resources could be exported, great wealth began to flow out of the area. And not much of it ever flowed back.

By the time I was born, nearly a century after the sinking of the pit, the valley I was to come to know so intimately in childhood had its hillsides piled high with coal slag, the waste product of a hundred years of toil by hundreds of thousands of men deep down in the narrow coal seams reached from the pithead of Merthyr Vale Colliery. The tips were shaped either conically, like black volcanoes, or were laid out in broad strips, following the contours of the mountain sides, just as the houses did. They were heaped up, endlessly, by a system of conveyor belts and 'drams' that ran from the colliery, clanking and rumbling around the villages all day long. Some of the volcano shapes were impossibly steep and piled so high that their tops rivalled in altitude the natural mountains on whose sides they had been dumped.

Coal had originally been extracted here to feed the ironworks at Cyfarthfa and Dowlais, after the area had been deforested and the supply of charcoal had been exhausted, and new technology came along that allowed the smelting of iron using coke. The steam coal extracted at Merthyr Vale fuelled thousands of steam engines as they drove the industrial revolution. It powered the Royal Navy and the Merchant Navy through the decades of Empire and for the duration of two world wars. By the 1960s it was being fed into power stations and was still being used for domestic heating in almost every home. All this while, day by day, the tips had grown larger and their summits higher.

All coal mining areas across the world have produced such tips but the South Wales coalfield is unusual, geologically, because it is also mountainous with next to no flat ground available for dumping. If you look today at old photographs of the mountainsides as they used to be, it seems ludicrous that anyone could have thought such a situation either sustainable or safe, with ribbons of terraced houses, shops, hospitals and schools dwarfed by the monstrous tonnages heaped up on steep slopes, right above them. Purest black, these tips loomed over our homes in defiance of gravity and of common sense. And they were everywhere. The tip that eventually collapsed and sent hundreds of thousands of tons of semi-liquid slurry careering into Aberfan was called Pantglas No. 7. And Pantglas was just a small part of Aberfan, Aberfan just one of hundreds of villages in the shadow of similar slag heaps, right across the South Wales coalfield.

But the fact that the two villages existed at all was by reason of the colliery. The villages existed because of the coal, and the coal fed them and fuelled them and kept them. Despite the coming of new factories to the valley in the 1950s and 1960s, at least one man in every family was, or at least had once been, a miner, and the miners' wages still underpinned the local economy. For most people the degradation of the environment was a necessary evil, the price of coal and the price of the jobs that were the foundation stones of every house, chapel, shop and pub for miles around.

At that time at least one coal fire still blazed in every house at all times of the day aside from the warmest days of summer. On windless days the coal smoke of a couple of thousand chimneys would hang in the still air and could be tasted like a hint of acid at the back of your throat. The effluent of coal washing turned the River Taff black, and choked almost all life from it.

The drive to extract coal meant its waste was amassed around us and was channelled through our waterways, and that the air we breathed was filled by the products of its burning. Yet it was also the reason for everything I knew being as it was. The reason all the people I knew, all the people I loved, were there at all.

The colliery itself sat at the heart of everything. Never truly quiet at any time of day or night, it clanked, rumbled, hissed and whistled. The steam hooter sounded at change of shift and steam shunting engines fussed endlessly over getting the coal wagons organised for the trip to Barry docks. At the top of its winding towers, its two pairs of winding wheels turned perpetually, day after day, year after year, with a deep whirring sound; the weight-driven pulleys of the villages' clockwork heart. At night the floodlights of the pit yard threw light across the ceiling of my bedroom at the back of our house. Aberfan was never completely dark, and never silent. Once, on a family holiday to Cardiganshire, in a rented cottage deep in the countryside, I found I could not sleep, so disconcerted was I by the quiet and the deep darkness of the fields and woods round about us. It seemed like a place without a heartbeat. At least none that I could then hear.

So this was the place I was born into: a pit village. Like all pit villages, it was characterised by the culture that the miners themselves had created; warm, supportive, egalitarian. There was a respect for education, for skills and hard work. To name someone 'a good worker' was the highest form of praise. The social activism of the miners and the fruits of a thousand of their incremental victories, alongside the work of the churches and chapels, formed the warp and weft of the community's fabric. The mighty National Union of Mineworkers was always working in the background, not on planning the next strike as some newspapers would have their readers believe, but as a legal and financial adviser to families and pensioners, a patron of sports and social clubs, a refuge for the victimised; even as a travel agent, should you fancy a jaunt to the seaside.

Of course, this was never any kind of utopia. There were enmities, jealousies and worse. The respect for education was undermined by a belief that many were not fitted for it, at least beyond school leaving age. And there were always some who never subscribed to the way the miners might seek to order things. This was a real place and not some working class Eden, and it was peopled by real human beings, with all their faults and frailties. But there was an ethos, made in those villages and particular to them, an ethos of trust and connectedness between people, forged under pressure, that would be honoured, always. This was something I only recognised and understood through its absence – when I left Aberfan at the age of eighteen to study at Edinburgh University, and was transplanted to a strange city, hundreds of miles away. When this happened I became suddenly disorientated by the seeming absence of shared assumptions about how community, society, ought to be. I felt like someone who makes to climb a staircase in the dark, only to stumble over a missing step, with a sudden nauseating lurch. I was disorientated too by the change in topography. Suddenly in a city with grand vistas that drew the eye toward the sea, or to distant hills, I realised that the valley I grew up in may well have been scarred by industry but it was also a natural shelter from the wider world, its mountains forming an embrace around the mind; protective, but enclosing too. Leaving the smothering warmth of that affectionate embrace was to be the hardest part of growing up.

After the disaster, Aberfan was still a pit village, no more or less than all the others. But there were differences too. In face of that unspeakable horror, it instinctively used its strengths to fight back. A close community grew closer. An organised community amplified and multiplied its organisations. The instinct for mutual support kicked in. But there were gaps, gaps that some would fall through. After all, how could a community that dealt with communal threats by communal means stand up to individual grief? How could any organisation, no matter how sensitive and well meaning, step in and give any answer to the boundless loss of a unique and irreplaceable child?

Today we might have called in experts in bereavement, psychologists perhaps, and counsellors. But in 1966, such things were not so well understood. So Aberfan in the aftermath of disaster became different. A community so strong in its connectedness was nevertheless undermined by the aching grief of parents, siblings, families and loved ones. The grief gnawed away at happiness, at peace of mind, at health, at hope. I grew up in this aftermath. After 21st October 1966, Aberfan was all about aftermath. The disaster was ever-present, like a vibration in the air, like that sense of unease when a dark shape flits about in the corner of your eye, like a spider scuttling along a skirting board.

This, then, was the atmosphere around us all in my pre-school years. The day of the disaster itself had carved itself into my memory at an age so tender I had no right to remember anything of it at all and the aftermath of that day permeated all the stages of my growing up. Just as my horizons broadened gradually, day by day as I grew, so an understanding of what that day had meant revealed itself in stages, piece by poignant piece. The two things could not be separated. To grow up in Aberfan at that time was to grow up with a shadow cast over all, mostly unacknowledged, but its presence felt through hushed adult conversation, overheard and partly understood; through the television and newspapers and their coverage of each anniversary of the day, through the gradual realisation that kindly adults you knew by name were also bereaved parents, and had suffered things far beyond anything your childish experience could prepare you to understand.

In those years before school, our home in Cottrell Street was the centre of my very restricted world. My parents were able to afford the £150 to buy the house because Dad's savings of £100 had been supplemented by the enormous windfall of £50 that Mam had won at bingo. A mid terraced, three-bedroom house just like all the others in the street. At first Mam, Dad, Anne, Allyson and I (Gareth had not yet been born when we first moved in and I was still the baby) had to share the house with a sitting tenant. An elderly lady by the name of Mrs Miles, she occupied the downstairs front room and I remember very little about her except that she terrified me. I can picture her now only as an unsmiling figure in a severe black dress. I have a fragment of memory that had me blundering once just a couple of steps into her musty smelling room – I must have only been beginning to learn to walk. There was a glass-fronted display cabinet against the wall to my right, and I came face to face at eye level with a black, perhaps jet, figurine behind the glass. It had a leering, grinning face. It looked to me like the very essence of evil and I recoiled from it, running away and weeping for my mother.

Upstairs, I was wary of the trap door to the attic. I knew that it was dark up there, and dusty, and no one lived there but spiders and silverfish. When I walked along the landing I was always careful not to walk directly under it, lest it suddenly spring open and shower me with old, dead husks of insects and skittering spider legs.

There were these dark corners of the house, but I always felt safe and secure, so long as my parents were there to watch out for me.

At the heart of every home in those days was the fire in the middle room. In our house, Mam was always first to get up in the morning in order to set it. She did this every day for years on end. She was the first to tackle the cold and dark on winter mornings, warming our clothes on a clothes horse near the fire. On waking each morning I would, at first, cling to the warmth beneath my blankets, aware of the freezing air in the bedroom as it pinched at my nose, reluctant to quit the perfect warmth under the covers. Only when I really had to would I break out from the warm pocket of the bed, padding downstairs as quickly as I could to make it to the living room where Mam had dulled the sharp edge of cold for the rest of us.

Given the chance, I would study with fascination the adult, alchemical skill of fire lighting. First the inky pages of the *Daily Mirror* or the *Merthyr Express* crumpled into balls, and then over that, the kindling that dad had split with a hatchet some time before. Then the lumps of coal on top. The paper was lit with a Swan Vesta and flared up and then, with a flourish, a sheet of outstretched newspaper was applied across the opening of the fireplace to draw the fire; the taut paper straining and charring alarmingly as the flames roared up behind it. Then the paper was whisked aside to reveal the finished product – the coal fire burning, domesticated and calm.

The fire needed tending all day long and real experts, like my Dada, could prolong its life by having the coal burn twice; the second time as coke, or by banking up the fire with powdered 'small coal', seeming to smother the flames altogether, until the red glow slowly ate its way through the black blanket to breathe again. In the evenings we all gathered about the fireplace, legs outstretched, basking in the warmth, guarding against anyone blocking our view of the flames and 'taking all the heat'. Spending time alone in one's room was too uncomfortable a prospect to contemplate outside summertime, and so we spent our time together around the fire. Staring into the flames I saw pictures being moulded, then dissolved in the hypnotic warmth, a miniature geography of black continents slowly inundated by red seas, until bedtime was called.

Diversion was added when we eventually took possession of a rented black and white 'Rediffusion' television, a man calling at the door each week to take payment for it. It had a clunky Bakelite dial to change the channel, not on the TV itself but screwed into the windowsill, and there were letters around the dial instead of numbers, with far more letters than there were actual channels available. Turning the dial from 'D' to 'H' produced nothing but snow on the screen and a loud hissing sound; even so I tried it now and again, just in case. I immersed myself in children's TV programmes, starting out with *Andy Pandy*, *Bill and Ben* and *Trumpton* but soon graduating to much more grown up stuff like the stories of *Noggin the Nog,* each one with a hint of menace. I took in glimpses of a wider world, of other countries: *Casey Jones*, 'steamin' and a rollin'' across a dusty America; *The Flashing Blade* and the chateaux of France; *Skippy the Bush Kangaroo* in the Outback of Australia and *Flipper,* the dolphin swimming in the seas off a perpetually sunny Florida. It never occurred to me that these were places that could be visited. They were simply story lands.

During my first remembered winters, the middle room was the only truly warm room in the house. Even our lean-to bathroom, newly constructed by my father and grandfather, and which boasted a shiny new electric fire on the wall with a string pull to switch it on and off, had an ineradicable chill; at least until Dad laid hands on a second hand paraffin heater which hissed and popped and gave off a chemical stink as it squatted in the corner of the room. Even so, the wet heat of the burning paraffin and the coldness of the walls and the metal framed frosted windows, formed streams of condensation that bred black mould that clung to the walls in huge quantities, spreading like a contagion. This horrified my eldest sister Anne so much she took to scrubbing obsessively at it with a nail brush dipped in neat bleach. When that didn't work, she persuaded Mam and Dad to let her paint over the mould. From heaven only knows where she managed to source a tin of lurid orange paint of a shade that could only have existed in the Seventies, which she had up on the walls and drying before our parents had a chance to veto the choice of colour. From that day on, sitting in the bath at Cottrell Street was like squatting at the centre of an enormous illuminated pumpkin.

The fussing and the grafting to capture warmth and carry little bundles of it with you was most urgent at bedtime. Mam would warm our pyjamas by the fire and then boil the kettle to fill three earthenware hot water bottles sitting on the kitchen table like fat brown piglets. Each of them wrapped in a towel, she would slip them between the sheets of our beds and leave them a while to work their magic through the blankets, sheets and mattresses. When bedtime came the best tactic was a swift sprint through the frigid bedroom air to dive into the little pocket of warmth left behind by the hot water bottle, and then to pull the weight of the blankets up to just under your nose. I shared my room with Gareth, then still in his cot. Each night the pit yard sounded its lullaby for us. It may well have been dirty and noisy and relentless, but I thought of the colliery as a kind of sentinel against the dark. There was always someone awake on the pit yard. Always someone alert. If anything went wrong while we slept, they would know and they would put it right. As it vibrated with energy, the mine's reassuring night light never failed. Our house, and all the houses in the tangled ribbons of the streets around, seemed watched over, always, as we settled for the night.

During that winter of 1966 we children were kept close. Each morning, my oldest sister Anne set off for the grammar school in Quakers Yard, three miles away by train and so far away and unknowable to me that I paid the idea of it no mind. Dad went off to work at the Hoover factory in Pentrebach. He was an engineer. Good work in a community that respected skills and qualifications. Mam, while we children were young, had her hands full at home, though she would later graft her way to a career in nursing once we were old enough for Nana (my father's mother) to mind us.

For Allyson there was no school for what seemed like a long time. Not until some prefabricated buildings were thrown together in another part of the village, and the survivors of Pantglas School restarted their lessons. One day a picture of Allyson speaking with the Queen appeared in all the newspapers. In the picture, my sister looks dazed and perplexed, far from comfortable. She has her best coat on. Mam made a cutting from the newspaper and put it away, without remarking on it, as if it were something that could not be made sense of just then but might have meaning sometime, for someone.

Around this time the clean-up operation began in earnest around Pantglas School and Moy Road, where several houses had been flattened by the landslide. Mechanical diggers worked all day and through floodlit nights. For a while the industrial clatter and illuminated night sky rivalled the activity of the pithead itself. Tens of thousands of tons of slurry had to be moved. Endless convoys of lorries rolled in and out of the village all day long, diesel engines thrumming and barking. Slowly the worst of the debris in the immediate area of the school and what had been Moy Road was cleared. The great black curve of slurry, cloying and menacing, was beaten back a little way. Even so, the remaining bulk of the tip itself, and all the other tips beside, remained exactly as they had been.

After the initial numbing shock of 21st October began to subside, anger and controversy began to take its place. The people of the two villages began a campaign to have the tips removed. Many spent sleepless nights, especially during rainy weather, straining their hearing for the sound of another landslide. The National Coal Board refused to pay for the clean-up. So did the government. Eventually the fury of the villagers and the incredulity of the public at large set the lorries and diggers to work on the tips themselves, but not before the disaster fund, made up of donations from thousands of sympathisers from around the world, had been raided by government to cover half the cost.

I remember the anger, humming through adult conversation like the vibrating string of a musical instrument. At the time it was disconcerting for me. I had little understanding of why so many adults sounded so bitter in their tone. Looking back on that time through adult eyes, however, I am glad it was there. Not just because the removal of the tips was a moral necessity in itself, but also because it implied the willingness, surviving in the hearts of many, to begin shaping a future for Aberfan and Merthyr Vale; a future free of fear of a repetition of that landslide, but also free of these great black middens of industry. Once people begin to talk and think about the future again, that which is past can sometimes, at least, begin to be borne. Those who at times cannot summon up the inner resources to articulate any case for the future, so beaten down are they by the pain of the past, become for that time possessed by the past, immobilised by it. The anger over the clearance of the tips was the first sign that the villages were not entirely eaten up, used up, by trauma. They still had fire.

That is not for a moment to pretend that grieving became

easier or that loss was any less bitter. Grief had taken up permanent residence in many hearts. Grief might ebb and flow and change its shape and appearance as the years come and go, but it never really leaves; never calls it quits. Only the realisation that love is just as permanent, just as bloody-minded, can balance out grief's corrosion of the human spirit.

The outside world came to Aberfan in force in those months after The Disaster, as the events of 21st October came to be known. As children we were sheltered from the bulk of it, and thankfully it meant little to us. Royalty, politicians, journalists and writers, churchmen and photographers, all came to the village. Some came to see and console. Some had wisdom enough to simply witness, and respect enough to simply show the world the reality of what had happened. Some tried to understand, to properly ask the question: 'how was this allowed to happen?'. But there were others with much lower motivations; knowing that tragedy sold newspapers, and caring for nothing else. Allyson while out playing was asked by a reporter to 'think about her dead friends' while a photograph of her was taken, so that she would have a suitably sad expression on her face. The reporter did not know that Allyson was in that particular part of the village where he had met her, away from our street, only because she had wandered far in search of someone her own age to play with, and that she had failed to find anyone. No doubt if he had known, he would have sold that fact too, along with her image.

And so interpretations of Aberfan's tragedy were printed in newspapers around the world and reports were made for broadcast. People of consequence, people with voices that would be listened to, visited, and their words recorded. In far greater numbers though, came people from other Valley communities. They dressed in their best out of respect and walked slowly around the area of Pantglas School and the demolished houses of Moy Road. They trod carefully and kept a discreet distance. They asked no questions, conducted no interviews, took no photographs; just simply saw. They took in the picture before them, so that they would remember it. They witnessed the clean-up operation, which was to last for years afterwards, the heavy machinery rumbling night and day amongst the slurry which curled its great black arm across the site of what was once classrooms and homes. The sight of Pantglas School, torn up. I like to think that they held their children a little more tightly than usual afterwards, when they got home.

The people of the village worked hard to keep the children clear of all this, as much as they could, though it was impossible not to feel the brokenness of things, even for a child as young as I was. Conversations between Mam or Dad and other adults at home or in the street would, all of a sudden, switch to whispers, and there would be sotto voce queries about how so-and-so was 'coping'. That word 'coping' I heard repeated over and over as the village conversed with itself endlessly in the months after. It gave voice to a desire to care and reach out, combined with a fear of intrusion into private grief. It was the euphemism adopted by all.

'Not too good,' would come the answer or, 'Yes, well, you know.'

When I went walking along Aberfan Road with Mam or Dad, they would, on multiple occasions, be held up in conversation with neighbours and friends, sometimes many times, before we reached our destination. I grew used to holding one or other of my parents' hands and waiting for the whispers to subside, impatient as children are. The whispers seemed to go on for such a long while, the patience of the adults around me seemingly limitless. It was as if through talking, through enquiring after those they knew, they sought to weave a kind of blanket out of softly spoken words; a blanket to wrap around themselves and the ones they spoke of, to keep away the harshness of an icy wind.

# Street Life

Despite all, the spring came and then the summer, and our front door stood permanently open and our street came to life.

Cottrell Street runs long and level, a single terrace, and we were the third house along from the end – even though we were number 2 – for reasons it didn't occur to me to ask about just then. Stone the Butcher's slaughterhouse stood right opposite us, taller than our house and showing us its blank side wall, blocking any view to the front of our house. It had been some while since it was actually used for slaughtering sheep and pigs, but it still housed the machine that made Stone's marvellous sausages. The butcher's shop itself was just five doors up, on our side of the street.

Next door to the slaughterhouse stood Rees the Undertakers, with old Mr Rees' coffin-making workshop alongside and its stone-cold cellar underneath. Bald as a billiard ball, taciturn, pale-skinned and stick thin, Mr Rees appeared appropriately cadaverous given his choice of profession, even when he wasn't burying anyone. On funeral days he wore a shiny black top hat and a black tail coat. Rumour had it that Mrs Rees was as bald as her husband, but I couldn't tell for sure if it was a wig or not; if it was, I certainly never saw her without it. The local boys would drive the Reeses potty by kicking footballs against the wall of the slaughterhouse, producing a repetitive booming thud-thud, which brought out Mrs Rees to yell at them about her nerves. This inevitably spurred the boys on to attempts at comedy: 'Don't worry Mrs Rees, your customers will sleep right through.' And to even greater efforts with the ball: thud-thud.

Next to Mr Rees' workshop was a small triangle of public land, just a few square yards of it. It was fenced off from the road and two public benches stood there on the pavement with the initials of every teenager in Aberfan carved into their wooden slatted seats. Inside the fence was a shallow stream and a couple of trees. These would be the first trees I would ever climb, and as I got to know them well, I could make it easily and quickly to the topmost branches. Often I'd perch there, hidden by the foliage and unseen, watching the world go by.

At the end of the street on our side of the road was the squat rectangular bulk of the Aberfan cinema, its art deco grandeur already fading fast, and opposite that, at the bottom of Bridge Street, was J&J's Garage with its BP sign; yellow letters on a green shield. Next door to J&J's stood the small, stone-built Zion Primitive Methodist chapel: our chapel.

This huddle of buildings, at the end of a nondescript terraced street, just like thousands of others in the South Wales Valleys, covered a patch of ground no more than perhaps a hundred yards by twenty; and it was my first entire world.

That first summertime I can remember, the summer of 1967, when I was three and a half years old, this small patch of the outside world was unveiled to me in fearful, fascinating glimpses as I took up station sitting on our front step, gawking nervously at the older kids as they filled the street with the speed and clamour of their games.

Outside school time on any fine day, the street was always

filled with fun and fury. The boys barged and shoulder-charged their way through games of football or of 'touch' with frequent stops for celebration, argument, and the loud mockery of losers. Or they would fire make-believe bullets at their enemies with two extended fingers to make a pistol: DATT-CHY! or wink down the barrel of an imaginary rifle whilst lying on the ground, sniper style: PAT-CHOWWW! or slaughter the opposition with an invisible Sten gun, shooting from the hip: DRRRRR-ATTTCHYY! The ricochet of bullets was a constant backdrop to our games, steeped, as we still were, in the stories of the war we read in the comics we avidly collected and swapped.

I was much too small to join in, and contented myself with my role as spectator. I did not see how I could ever match the size and strength of these boys with their scabbed, bony knees and breakneck turns of speed. Some even had daps to wear for playing outdoors, not just sandals like me.

The girls' games were much more sophisticated and elaborate. Sometimes they played with double skipping ropes, seven feet long, whirling at high speed as they maintained a clacking rhythm, the ropes and the girls' shoes tapping at the road. The rope swingers whirled their ropes and chanted rhymes as those doing the actual skipping danced first into the bewildering blur and then out again, the aim being not to miss your timing or hit the ropes:

'Keep the kettle boiling,
miss a beat you're out'.

How they managed this, time after time without mishap, flummoxed me completely. The ropes were swinging far too fast to be seen. So I decided that this skill must be something taught solely and secretly to girls, passed on from one generation to the next in clandestine conversations. It was for girls, I reassured myself, so I needn't worry about it anymore.

If not skipping, the girls played hopscotch, chalking numbered boxes on the pavement and sliding a stone with their shoe, hopping from box to box, or they plaited cats cradles of ever increasing elaboration with stretchy strings of huge length made with dozens and dozens of joined-up elastic bands, stretched between two sets of ankles. Or they would juggle against the slaughterhouse wall with two old tennis balls, fuzzy coatings long since worn away, the balls tapping, keeping time with the rhythm of their chanting:

'Nebuchadnezzar the King of the Jews
Bought his wife a pair of shoes
When the shoes began to wear
Nebuchadnezzar began to swear
When the swear began to stop
Nebuchadnezzar bought a shop
When the shop began to sell
Nebuchadnezzar bought a bell
When the bell began to ring
Nebuchadnezzar began to sing...'

The street was alive, always, with people. First to call in the morning was Jacky-the-milk, his horse and cart recently updated to motorised transport, silver top and gold top milk bottles chinking. Orders clunked on doorsteps, empties collected, and tat-tat-tat on doors once a week for payment.

Shortly after the milk round came the baker's van from Troedyrhiw with its still-warm and aromatic cargo of cobs, 'Swanseas', tin loaves, baps, and Hovis wrapped in greaseproof paper. Women gathered at the open doors at the back of the van to talk, tease, and be teased.

Once a week the costermonger threw open the back doors of his high-sided green van to unleash the smell of cabbage leaves, fresh damp earth and citrus peel, and to reveal a welter of Pembrokeshire potatoes, muddy carrots, swedes, parsnips, and onions tied in bunches. In the summer this smell would be overlaid by the sugar-ripe fragrance of strawberries in punnets, oozing juice, the sharp acid tang of sticks of rhubarb that were longer than I was tall, and the heady fresh odour of tubs of fat raspberries. In autumn would come crisp scented apples; Russets and Worcesters and Golden Delicious.

There was a weekly call from a fishmonger too, van doors flung wide open to let loose the smell of the sea, with trays full of cod, hake, and winkles, tubs of cockles to eat with a safety pin, and strips of lurid-yellow smoked haddock, as long as my arm, flung onto a weighing scale and parcelled up in newspaper for purchase.

The last of the horse drawn traders arrived just once a month at evening time using not the road, but our back *gwli*, horse's hooves clopping, his nasal cry of, 'Any old raaag-bone!' carrying for miles.

Betwixt and between and more infrequently, came the more exotic, unusual, door-to-door sellers: the knife-and-scissor-sharpening man with his portable whirring whetstone, who could sharpen garden shears too if you had some. The umbrella repair man who worked with a pair of sharp-nosed pliers while standing at your door, and gypsy women and children selling clothes pegs and pinches of lucky white heather tied with green ribbon.

All these callers punctuated the days, weeks and months of my early childhood with their daily door knock, their teasing and their jokes. As reliable as a railway timetable, they seemed a permanent feature of what our street was, how it was, in its seemingly indestructible being. Through their timetabled presence and their work, people were connected with the outside world, if only briefly, by being brought a little way beyond their own front door each and every day. If a door was not answered, they noticed and asked a neighbour why, and what was up. No matter how determined a misanthropist you might be, this was a place where it was near impossible to live or die entirely alone.

I had no conception of how fragile it all was. This way of doing business door-to-door could only last so long as most households had someone at home in daytime, so long as one wage was enough to keep a family, and whilst hardly anyone had access to a car. So of course, all these door-to-door trades were shortly – very shortly – to die away. Now that they have, our doors stay closed, like as not the whole day long, and a knock on the door has become viewed all too often as a disturbance, an intrusion even, where once it was a necessity and an enlivenment of every day.

The closest proper shop to our house declared its line of business by means of a deeply carved marble slab set behind its window, letters picked out in shiny dark blue paint: 'Stone: Family Butcher'. Phyllis and Gertie Stone, the elderly sisters who owned the premises and another beside, lived above the shop, and as far as I was concerned they must have been rich since they owned the only private telephone in the street, maybe even the whole village. Phyllis and Gertie kept themselves to themselves however, and were rarely seen. The shop was run single-handedly by their employee, Arthur the butcher.

Arthur was everything a butcher ought to be. Red faced and... well-fed, let's say. He was quick to smile and joke and was permanently swathed around his ample middle in a blue and white striped apron. He kept a pencil stub behind his ear, extricating it from time to time to add up a customer's bill on the corner of the paper used to wrap their purchase. Arthur, in short, was a Ladybird book illustration of a butcher. He hacked and sliced and chopped his way through the day, starting early each morning by making sausages in the slaughterhouse, and then setting about ensuring that his cornucopia of a window display was ready for the customers and second-to-none in its neat, crowded magnificence. The window was soon crammed with serried ranks of lamb and pork chops, slices of brawn and tongue, haslet and ham. Chickens were piled in pyramids, like acrobats petrified in mid performance, threatening to topple into slick red-brown lakes of liver and puddles of kidneys. Trays of faggots fought for space with joints of beef, and a disembodied pig's head was set centre stage, to watch over all the rest, grinning at some private joke between Arthur and itself. Set all around and between were miniature hedgerows of bright green plastic parsley. Most impressive of all, as far as I was concerned, dangling from hooks on the white tiled walls, were yard upon yard of Arthur's speciality – his home-made sausages, linked and knotted in fat, fleshy chains and best eaten, in my experience, straight from the frying pan on the end of a fork, still hot enough to burn the tip of your tongue.

Some years later, when I had grown a little older, a bunch of us boys would make the trip to Arthur's domain now and then in search of contraband goods.

'What you after now then, boys?' he'd ask, knowing fine well why we had come. Whilst the rest of us looked down, avoiding eye contact and making little furrows in the sawdust on the quarry tiled floor with the toes of our shoes, the eldest amongst us would be nudged into action:

'You got any, Arthur?'

'I don't know, I don't know,' he protested. 'Your mothers will be in here now, telling me what for.'

'We won't tell, Arthur, honest,' we piped up, ludicrously enough, since what we had come for could have had only one possible source.

Then with a theatrical rolling of eyes and the hint of a knowing smirk, Arthur would retreat into the back room and re-emerge with a small loosely wrapped paper parcel. Necks were craned as he peeled back the paper to reveal the grisly contents: a collection of dismembered pigs' tails and chickens' feet. Re-wrapped and handed over, Arthur would giggle as we bolted from the shop to divide the spoils.

Now the chickens' feet and pig tails weren't for eating, of course. We valued them for another reason. Their capacity to scare girls. Especially sisters.

The chickens' feet were best, because they could be brought back to life. Pinching and yanking the tendon in the bloody end of the leg would make the toes and claws clench into a cold, dead fist. This was entertainment enough in itself, but the real fun was to be had by creeping up behind an unsuspecting victim, setting the foot gently on the shoulder and yanking the tendon sharply, and then standing back in triumphant satisfaction as a screaming girl – with a disembodied chicken's foot firmly attached to her jumper – bolted in a blind panic. My eldest sister Anne was the best possible victim of this ploy as she was permanently trusting, no matter what evidence to the contrary the world might throw at her, and was so easily spooked that even the sprig of green at the top of a tomato, when dropped into her lap, would have her screaming in the belief that it was a spider.

'Get it off. Get it off. Nooooo!' she'd scream.

This tormenting of the opposite sex was somehow considered natural then, and part of the job description of being a boy. I should now apologise. At long last. In writing.

Our street, back then, was a living thing; far more than simply a collection of houses. It was filled with people's comings and goings. Neighbours were summoned by calling down their hallway through their open door, since visiting required no pretext and no appointment. This was where the grown-ups gathered for news and gossip and, in good weather, it was a place to linger and take an aimless stroll, or even to pull up a chair. Tumults of children bowled in and out of doorways and watching over them, and if need be telling them off, was the accepted role of any adult that happened to be near. The street was an open air extension of all our homes, used in common. It seemed secure, it seemed entirely safe, it seemed blessed. With a child's certainty I knew it must have been always like this, and it always would be.

I saw another side to things though, the time my father took me along one winter evening to visit our immediate neighbours, Mr and Mrs Owen who lived next door to us at Number 1.

Number 1, Cottrell Street, had once been a fish and chip shop, but by this time the now elderly couple that owned it had grown too frail to keep it running. They had asked for my Dad's help to fix a fuse. I remember it was growing dark and raining hard, water sloshing down through the downpipe of the slaughterhouse across the road. We entered through the front door which led to the now defunct shop area where the old counter and deep fat fryer stood right in front of us. Both were covered with a thick layer of dust, as was the floor of bare boards. There was a strong smell of mustiness and damp and, from the old fryer, a sharp tang of rancid oil and fat. The walls were greasy and streaked with dirt. There was no light save that cast by the orange glow of the new sodium street lamp at the corner of the street together with a dim illumination through the crack of a door left ajar behind the counter. I felt uneasy, disorientated. This place had a feeling of emptiness, more like an abandoned building than a home. I looked back through the old shop front window to see needles of relentless rain illuminated by the new street lamp. Dad called out to announce our presence, our footsteps echoing in the empty space as we walked straight through to the back room. The old couple had, it seemed, in their so-called retirement, taken refuge here, just leaving their old workplace behind them.

Despite the fact that they lived right next door, I hardly knew the old couple, as they were rarely seen outside. I was already feeling awkward, as children often do when they meet new people. When I entered that back room with my father it was obvious that they must rarely have ventured anywhere beyond it. They seemed stranded, marooned here. They were huddled in two armchairs, their knees covered with blankets. Mrs Owen had a shawl about her shoulders. Their chairs were arranged in front of a single bar electric fire. The fire was not working – hence the appeal to my Dad, I supposed. They were both frail-looking and thin, both white-haired and with pale translucent skin. They seemed to me so impossibly old, and

the image flashed into my mind of a nursery rhyme book illustration I had seen of 'the little old woman who lived in a shoe'. In the book the old woman was walking with a stick, bent double. Until then I had thought my grandparents, then in their sixties, were as old as anyone could be. I now realised that wasn't true, after all.

'I won't get up, if you don't mind, David,' Mr Owen said to my father.

'Never you mind, Mr Owen,' my father said and rested his hand on the old man's shoulder, for just a second. He accepted the touch of my father's hand with a distracted nod, and breathed a barely audible sigh. 'Aye,' he said.

'How be, Mrs Owen?' asked Dad, raising his voice just slightly. She didn't answer or look up. Instead she took in a deep breath and nodded whilst keeping her watery-eyed gaze on the floor.

Apart from the armchairs, there was no other furniture in the room except for a rickety table with a stale half loaf and a bone-handled bread knife on it. There was an old style valve radio alongside, which was either switched off or no longer working. Rain was rattling hard on the tin roof of what must have been their kitchen in the space beyond. It sounded like the drumming of metallic fingers; cold, and indifferent to human concerns. This room was cold and wet. Not just damp. Wet. Tiny rivulets of water ran down the walls over what might once have been wallpaper, and collected in shallow puddles on the uneven floor which was only partly covered by mismatched strips of oilcloth worn thin and leached of any colour. Bare flagstones were visible through the gaps. The whole scene was lit dimly by the filament of a single bare light bulb, which was, at least, still burning. I drew my arms close to my body,

shrinking into myself, fearful of touching anything, or even brushing up against anything; as if there were something catching on every surface, in the very air. Then, realising what I was doing and a little ashamed, I tried to force myself to relax.

The smell within that room was new to me then, though in adulthood I grew to recognise it again. A miasma of staleness in the air, of unwashed bodies and unwashed clothes, of chill, of unspoken desperation. Unmistakable. It was the smell of poverty.

My father was scrupulously polite and respectful to them both, perhaps even more than he usually was with people, I thought. He introduced me to Mr and Mrs Owen quite formally, and Mr Owen extended his hand. I hesitated, nervous, reluctant.

'Your oldest boy, this is then?' he asked.

'That's right, this is young Huwcyn,' Dad said and flicked his head to the side to indicate I should shake the old man's hand. Something in my father's expression broke through my reluctance and I realised I was being ill-mannered. I took Mr Owen's hand. His skin was cold, but his handshake steady enough, and all of a moment the simple human touch of his hand taught me a silent little lesson. I think I cringed a bit inside, ashamed of my prior disdainful prissiness. I have never forgotten that lesson.

Dad asked after the old couple's health as he worked to fix the fuse using the fuse wire, wrapped around a little piece of cardboard that he'd brought with him.

'O, you know David. Can't complain, can't complain,' said Mr Owen in response. The truth did not need utterance.

My father then reached down to the electric point on the wall to switch the electric fire back on. I noticed that the flex

leading to the fire was the old-fashioned kind with brown, woven cotton insulation. It was frayed and trailed across the puddle strewn floor. Even as young as I was, I knew that was not right, but I said nothing, and Dad flicked the switch. Feebly, the element began to glow, emitting all the while a loud humming sound. It was pathetic, that fire. It would have been hell's own task for a dozen such to have warmed that room. The very masonry bled its frigidity into the air.

Before we left, Dad asked if the Owens needed anything else and Mr Owen was so quick to say, 'No, no David, we are just sorry to have bothered you. Thank you David.'

'Good night then, both,' Dad said.

'Good night, David,' he said. Mrs Owen nodded weakly again.

We walked back through the old shop and into the street. Outside it was still raining, still cold, but the night air now seemed wonderfully clean and fresh and I took deep draughts of it as if all the while, inside number 1, I had been holding my breath.

It was years later that it occurred to me to wonder why my father had taken me with him to see Mr and Mrs Owen at all. I was surplus to requirements; neither use nor ornament when it came to the fixing of fuses. Dad didn't offer any explanation at the time, and young as I was I simply accepted that he wanted me to go with him and that was that.

Now I think he just wanted to show me, and so teach me something words could not entirely convey. To have me witness how some people had to live.

When I was a little older, perhaps seven or eight years old, and able to wander with confidence a little further from the house,

Saturday mornings became matinee mornings at the Aberfan cinema which stood squat, and to my eyes gargantuan, at the end of our street. As soon as they were unlocked, dozens of us would push and jostle through the main swing doors into the foyer which smelled strongly of floor polish together with a hint of disinfectant. Here we bought our supplies to sustain us through the show; a small carton of squash and an orange. These were pretty much the only things sold in the cinema shop, aside from some elderly, faded yellow boxes of Rowntree's Fruit Gums displayed behind glass. These were far too expensive to buy and seemed to have remained unsold for a very, very long time. It occurred to me that they might not contain any actual fruit gums at all, and that they were simply for show.

Then it was through to the dusty half-light of the auditorium proper and the fight was on to sit as near to the back of the theatre as possible, not because of any improvement in our view of the screen, but because this gave tactical advantage. We drained the plasticky tasting orange squash as quickly as possible through the straw that came glued to the carton. The empty waxed cardboard container was now a grenade and our primary weapon.

'Fire!'

The cartons were hurled into the ranks of the enemy seated in the rows in front, shouts of approval rising for any good hit. Roars of joyous outrage would then precede a swift retaliation as the kids in the rows further forward now hurled their cartons – and ours – back at us. Ammunition rapidly ran low as the cartons bounced off seat backs and the tops of heads, to be lost in the semi-darkness. So, crouching down amidst the threadbare velvet seats that gave out little puffs of dust as they flipped back upright, we clawed at our oranges, ripping off the peel with a frantic sense of urgency lest the enemy get the drop on us. Jumping up out of cover we sprayed the seats in front with citrus smelling bullets, along with accompanying machine gun noises. Gradually, and with ill grace, the battle subsided a little as the lights faded out completely to leave the theatre lit only by the signs for the exit and the ladies and gents, since any further ammunition became impossible to find in the murk. And so we settled into the comfortable darkness which was filled with the powerful tang of orange zest and the ammoniacal whiff of pee as the toilet doors at the side of the stalls began to bang open and shut, as they ceaselessly would throughout the whole of the show.

These were the final days of the Saturday morning cinema serials. Batman and Robin took calls on the Batphone and KA-POW!-ed their way through Gotham City taking on the Penguin and the Joker after escaping the villains' over-elaborate plans to kill off the Dynamic Duo. Zorro defended the poor and swished a capital 'Z' on every wall he passed by, and Flash Gordon zoomed across the universe in implausible-looking rocket ships with fireworks for engines. Each of these shows were already old and had been shown over and over, but that was all incidental to the thrill of sitting in the communal dark whilst the projector's beam search-lighted the dust motes above our heads. I sat there on my musty-smelling flip-up seat wearing the green cable-knit jumper my grandmother had knitted for me, a pair of itchy grey shorts held up by the snake belt I was particularly proud of, ankle socks and sandals on my feet, and the taste of chemically enhanced orange squash in my mouth, entranced by the specialness of this darkness-in-daytime. It was entirely magical.

When the show was over a cataract of kids tumbled down the cinema steps and back into the startling daylight and the clamour of our games in the street and the *gwli*. Or we might jump the wall behind the cinema that separated off 'Dickie Rees's' from the Cottrell Street *gwli*. This was an area of waste ground piled with tumps of clinker waste from the breeze block making works at the other end of our street. There were three wrecked cars here, abandoned and left to rust. They were piled up together, one of them upside down, all the glass of their windscreens and windows long since shattered and lying as crystalline cubes all around. As far as we were concerned, these wrecked cars were heaven sent, a playground in themselves. We would clamber into the upturned car through a broken window into what was left of the interior which, despite its wrecked state, still had that car smell of imitation leather and engine oil. This interior could transform into anything; an aeroplane, a tank, a submarine or spaceship, and we would squabble for control of the upside-down steering wheel to pilot our imaginary craft, swinging it wildly from side to side and flicking switches on the dashboard to launch torpedoes, drop our bomb load, or fire deadly laser beams.

All around the cars, the waste clinker formed a gritty moonscape that begged to be explored, hidden in, or crawled through on your belly, commando style. Sometimes we fought elaborate war games here, and built forts on top of the tumps and raised flags made from scrap cloth and broom handles. Once we fought as the Cottrell Street Boys against the Barrington Street Boys, using dustbin lids for shields, sticks for swords, and hurling rocks at the opposition whenever they got within range. It was merciless and I wonder now that no one ever seemed to end up in hospital, or worse.

On one of those Saturday mornings I decided to head off on my own to explore the village a little further from home than usual. I felt drawn towards the site of Pantglas School, by then demolished, but still with the clamour of the heavy machinery, mechanical diggers and trucks engaged in the removal of slurry just uphill of the site, along the line of the old Merthyr to Cardiff canal. The roadway was still covered by a wet crust of black coal waste that was washed downhill whenever it rained. Just where the Aberfan community centre now stands, there was then an old garage that had been abandoned after the disaster. I decided to explore. Under the old corrugated iron roof the air was still and smelled powerfully of the engine oil that still slicked the concrete floor. There was an old car tyre lying about which I latched onto immediately as something to play with, and I began rolling it across the floor. It was so heavy that each time it lost momentum, spinning slowly to a wobbling standstill, it took a huge amount of huffing and puffing to right it and get it rolling again. Sweaty with effort, I gave it an extra powerful heave, and this time it rolled and disappeared over the edge of a mechanics' inspection pit in the middle of the floor, landing at the bottom with a loud rubbery thud. Annoyed at losing my plaything, and without thinking, I lowered myself down the side of the pit until my arms were completely outstretched and I was dangling from the edge with straining fingers. I had no choice then but to let go and I clattered to the bottom. Then I realised I was stuck. The vertical walls of the pit were too smooth to gain any purchase, and I was too small to reach the lip of the pit and drag myself out. I felt a flutter of panic in my chest. Inside this hole in the ground I could hear the sound of my rapid breathing echoing off the concrete walls and all I could see of the outside world was a rectangular section of the garage roof. The sounds of the diggers and lorries working nearby had become muffled. I felt suddenly cut off from the outside world. I tried a running jump to reach the top edge but it was no good, the walls surrounding me were too high, and I clattered against them, skinning knees and elbows. So then I rolled the tyre upright and propped it against the wall and tried to balance on top of it on tip-toe to reach the edge. This almost worked, and I managed to get my fingers hooked over the edge of the hole, but I ended up skinning my knees again as I slid back down to the bottom. The pit was too deep, its walls too smooth, but I had no choice but to try this again, and then again, though each time I was further and further from succeeding as my arms and legs grew tired and began to tremble from the effort. I was well and truly stuck. A sense of panic rose in me again and I fought the urge to cry. Almost as bad as the fear of remaining stuck was the mortal embarrassment of having been stupid enough to get down into this hole in the first place. It was this embarrassment that led me to delay the only option left open to me – to call for help. For some minutes I simply stared at the walls of my concrete prison cell and the faraway rectangle of ceiling and I breathed hard like an animal in a trap. Panic was beginning to set in. Eventually I had to do it.

'Hello! Help!'

My call sounded small and pathetic, like the mewling of a baby animal. I felt it must be swallowed up by the sides of the pit so that no one passing on the road outside could possibly have heard it. My panic grew and grew.

But I was wrong. Almost immediately the head and shoulders of a man wearing a Dai cap appeared above me.

'Well, now then sunshine,' he said, 'how in the hell did you manage this?'

I was too embarrassed to answer. The man squatted on the edge of the pit, reached down and hauled me up by my wrist in one easy movement. I remember his jacket smelled of beer and tobacco smoke. He had been, most likely, on his way home from the social club and a lunchtime pint. My shame at my own stupidity was so complete that I didn't even think to thank him for rescuing me and so I simply stood there staring at the ground, feeling mortified. And then he rescued me again by saying sternly:

'Straight home to your mother. Bloody kids.'

I belted off down the road as fast as I could. When I reached the safety of home I told no one of the incident at the inspection pit. I hoped the man who hauled me out would tell no one either. It was a long while before I went off to play on my own again.

That episode aside, and as was more usual, we eventually became exhausted by our Saturday morning games in the *gwli* and on the waste ground, and prompted by the calls of mothers from various back gardens, we would drift back home for our dinner – perhaps six penn'orth of chips from the chip shop on Aberfan Road served up with slices of tinned ham, all of it swimming in vinegar.

After lunch it was a choice – back out to the *gwli* again and more games, or settle down with the grown-ups to watch *Grandstand* on the telly, or Mick McManus wrestling on *World of Sport*. Pools coupons would be held in readiness for checking when the day's football results came in, clacking away on the teleprinter at the end of the afternoon, and there might be jelly and Ideal Milk for tea.

Each of these Saturdays seemed so long lasting, so set in permanence, that I had no conception at all that time would bear them away, taking me, the boy I was, along with them. I did not conceive, either, of the absences amongst the older kids as they played their games alongside us. We played heedlessly in the spaces left by those now forever absent. I thrived in the permanent present of childhood, the damage of the past going unheeded – and the future? Well, surely, that was to be simply a matter of reliving today?

I might have dreamed from time to time, and vaguely, of an adulthood in which I would make a great impact on the world – an heroic life as a scientist like Alexander Fleming, saving the lives of millions through insight and brilliance alone. Or as a people's champion like Aneurin Bevan demolishing injustice through eloquence and guile. But the lesson to be learned in time was this: it is not the impact we might make upon the world so much as the impact the world makes upon us that will make us what we are. And the world will always win.There is a doctors' surgery now where the cinema once was. New houses have been built on Dickie Rees' waste ground. Stone's butcher shop has closed long since. The costermonger's children do not follow in their father's footsteps. Even the bridge at the end of Bridge Street has gone.

Cottrell Street is still there, mind you, though it no longer echoes with the clamour of children's games. There are just cars instead, parked end-to-end.

# On the Seventh Day

Sundays were different in every way. A lie-in was essential, and I was generally awakened late by the sound of saucepans clanking on the gas cooker in the kitchen and the aroma of roast leg of lamb slowly unfurling itself through the house. Sometimes I would lie awake in bed for some while, listening to the muffled sounds of my parents busy in the kitchen, and simply wallow in the feeling of complete peace and security brought on by being here, at home, and needing nothing more. Days like that would open slowly, like a flower.

The making of Sunday dinner was always Dad's domain since, truth be told, Mam's culinary competence was questionable to say the very least. Even when she prepared toast under the grill it usually ended with her scraping off a layer of charcoal into the sink with a butter knife. Her cooking could even imperil life and limb. Amongst her few culinary specialities was 'boiled cake', a recipe which, I was to discover years later, was invented in America during the great depression when many ingredients, like milk and eggs, were hard or impossible to find. Even so, if finished off successfully, a boiled cake had the consistency of a dense fruit loaf, and wasn't really half bad. Mam's attempts tended to emerge from the oven encased in a hard black crust. Anne joked that we should sell Mam's boiled cake to the Ministry of Defence, as a new, unbreachable, form of armour plating, ideal in the construction of tanks.

Once, when attempting to fire up the gas oven to finish a boiled cake, armed with a Swan Vesta, she got too close, and with a loud 'whump!' the gas ignited and Mam emerged with her eyebrows burned completely away, though curiously with her beehive hairdo still intact. Although she was otherwise unhurt, her eyebrows never completely recovered.

'I bloody hate cooking,' she said quietly to herself.

Since lean roast meat was a Sunday only treat back then, and offal was cheaper, Mam often conjured up a weekday treats like fried kidneys, liver, or cold slices of tongue. More usual, though, was an offering of roast heart, one for each of us, stuffed with Paxo sage and onion stuffing mix and sewn shut with a needle and thread. Not so bad really, but the hearts more often than not ended up semi-cremated, lying shrivelled, scorched and hard in the baking tray like six black grenades. Mam let them drop with a near metallic clang onto our plates, one by one.

'I bloody hate cooking,' she'd say, under her breath.

So on Sunday mornings, for the greater security of all, and in the hope of an edible dinner, Dad did the cooking and Mam was delegated the task of preparing the mint sauce. Mint grew in everyone's garden at that time and bunches were torn up and the leaves picked off to form a little aromatic hillock in the centre of a saucer. The leaves were then chopped and chopped again with a double sided safety razor blade, and slowly reduced to a minty mush. Transferred to a small jug and made up with watered vinegar and a teaspoonful of sugar, there was the mint sauce for another Sunday. Even today, the heady smell of roast leg of lamb and mint sauce transports me back to those childhood Sunday mornings.

Before we could eat, however, there was Sunday School. In 1968, Methodist churches throughout Britain donated money in the wake of the disaster to Zion Primitive Methodist chapel at the end of our street, and with the money the tiny chapel was extended to the rear and a modern youth centre was tacked on to the old building with a flat roof and plate glass windows and bright fluorescent lighting. It looked to me like a spaceship huddled behind a prim old horse and cart. We children each in turn laid a foundation brick for the new building with our initials carved on it. I can remember now the weight of my particular brick – I had to use both hands to hold on to it – and my nervousness in trying to lay it straight and just so, for fear I'd make the whole new building crooked. The bricks supported a memorial window with the names of the Sunday School pupils who had died in Pantglas School inscribed on it. I never counted, but the number of bricks was about the same as the number of names on the glass.

Save for the old tin chapel on Aberfan Road, which was made from corrugated iron, and so not much more than a glorified shed, and in any case now long gone, Zion was the smallest chapel in the village. Today it is the only one. Each Sunday at 11am Allyson, Gareth and I were packed off across the road to it, leaving Dad to carry on bustling in the kitchen; soaking carrots with lashings of 'bicarb', wrestling enormous cabbages cut from my Dada's garden, chopping the leaves and leaving them to sit in briny water to divest them of their slugs. At the ready with flour, cabbage water and a bottle of Crosse & Blackwell gravy browning, he would ensure all would be prepared by the time we got back.

Walking through the small Gothic arched door of the little chapel and into the pale, still light amongst the pews meant, always, entering a place of greater calm. Always we would automatically lower our voices and slow to a walk without being bidden. The nonconformist interior was whitewashed and simple with a plain brass cross above the pulpit and the big seat. Each window niche held a brass vase filled with fresh cut chrysanthemums, and an old oak-cased wall clock tocked and ticked, always somehow a little more slowly and with greater deliberation than clocks found elsewhere. The smell of furniture polish, Brasso and old, dry paper permeated all.

The Reverend Penberthy, a Cornishman, led the service and we would launch into the first hymn: 'Jesus wants me for a Sunbeam', perhaps. One of our Sunday school teachers, Bronnie Gough, led the singing; tall and elegant, a shy woman with a gentle soul, Bronnie had a beautiful, tremulous, soprano voice that floated high above us and was at least some compensation for our childish squawking. Then the Lord's Prayer, still being learned, and a thruppenny bit for the wooden collection plate. Then it was time to break for 'lessons' and we passed through the door at the rear of the chapel and bounded up the steps into the brand new youth club beyond. The modernity of this building made for a different atmosphere. It had bright Formica-topped tables, vinyl floor tiles and orange stacking chairs smelling strongly of new plastic. Here we began to laugh and talk loudly, milling about as the kettle boiled for the grown-ups who acted as our Sunday School teachers. Eventually we settled down and we were separated into groups by age, each group in a different room. For the youngest, like me, our 'lesson' consisted of having a bible story read to us from the great fat Children's Bible with colour illustrations on every page, and afterwards we'd colour in a picture from the story, printed in outline on slips of paper, using vivid waxy crayons that smelled good enough to eat.

And so here, week by week, I learned of Eden, of Noah and the flood, of Daniel in the lions' den, of Abraham and Isaac, and of Shadrach, Meshach and Abednego in the midst of the burning fiery furnace; of tested faith, Pharaohs and Pharisees and the tragedy of truth unheeded. Our Sunday School teachers were patient, far from strident in their belief, and all the more convincing for it. Each one of them; June Vaughan, Mr Williams, Mrs Iverson and Bronnie Gough, exuded a calm and gentle form of faith that fixed my attention and drew my respect. Even today I think enviously of their understated spirituality. The bible stories gripped my imagination and I travelled with them through the sun-scorched, cruel days of Ancient Egypt into Israel and Judah and the times of the prophets. All was as it should be in this ancient past, it seemed to me then; an immovable foundation to our young present, its truths rendered indelible in primary coloured, wax crayon.

When lessons were done, it was back to the chapel proper where Reverend Penberthy conducted us through the highlight of the service by telling us one of his 'stories-with-a-moral' which usually featured a diminutive hero he'd invented called 'Dicky Blackbird', who got into scrapes but always learned his lesson in the end. Reverend Penberthy sang a song of his own composition to finish, and accompanied himself on a vast, shiny piano accordion, all ebony black and mother of pearl. It gleamed like a miniature Cadillac.

Then it was the Apostle's Creed, a prayer said with our eyes clamped shut and finally the Dismissal: 'The Lord bless you and keep you, the lord make his face to shine upon you… and give you peace'. And often, in that moment, peace there was.

But then the service was over and it was time to head home and we made for the door, trying hard not to run until we got outside.

We ran back over the road and crashed through our front door. Home again, and time for Dad's lamb dinner with Mam's mint sauce. The highlight of the week, particularly if washed down with Corona red pop, fizzing in its glass tumbler like chemicals in a test tube. Seconds were always available and Gareth and I would quarrel over the bones from the joint to pick clean, and we worried out the marrow with our tongues.

After dinner, most Sunday afternoons were set aside for visiting my grandparents. My mother's parents, known to us grandchildren as Nan and Dad Pierce, lived in Bryn Teg Terrace, across the river in Merthyr Vale. Bryn Teg was a man-made cliff face of a street and the most elevated in the village. Each house was reached at the front by about twenty precipitous stone steps, and the street stretched along what was then the main road between Merthyr and Cardiff, which was, even in those days, too busy with traffic to play on. Their front doorstep gave a panoramic view of both our sibling villages and of Merthyr Vale pit which seemed to clank and whirr much louder when heard from here than it did in Cottrell Street. To the rear, just across the narrowest of alleyways, which you could span with your outstretched arms, sprang up the great bulk of Merthyr Vale mountain, as steep as any alp. A monstrous, sandstone retaining wall strained, buckled, and occasionally partly failed to hold back the enormous compression caused by the mountain's natural inclination to fold itself back into the cut that had been made to build the houses. After rain, water oozed between its stones, eroding the mortar and slowly winning the battle the hillside waged to heal itself, no matter how many repairs might be made. The whole street clung to the hillside in defiance of geology, living on borrowed time since being thrown together quickly and cheaply by the coal owners less than a century before. It was not built to last. Nor did it, in the end.

David and Mary Pierce were Welsh-speaking north Walians blown south by the winds of economic necessity sometime in the 1920s. Like the seeds of two tough mountain plants, they clung to this southern hillside but, like their house, they were never quite comfortable with their location. They raised eight surviving children in that house at number 16, but spoke of this part of Wales, if they spoke of it at all, as if it were an accidental destination they had stumbled upon, finding it both an enigma and a disappointment. Their thoughts and conversation always turned stubbornly northwards, drawn like a compass needle by the magnetism of their ever-present homesickness. They talked of Snowdonia and Lleyn and of their youth, lived amongst the clean beauty of the mountains and seashore and holy villages of Merionethshire, far away from the coal slag and smoke of the South. Like Bryn Teg itself, it was as if they had been placed here in error and they seemed to be anxious, always, for the error to be righted. They held their memories close, and doted on them. Their use of Welsh they kept for themselves alone, and they never spoke the language in front of even their children let alone us grandchildren; it had travelled with them from home, and they kept it like a treasure in a box, locked inside with their memories, retrieving it only when they thought no-one else was in earshot.

On these Sunday visits we would sit gathered in their tiny middle room. Dad Pierce in his chair, always with a bottle of whisky discreetly near (though I never saw him in drink) and on the oilcloth-covered table the pools coupon for next week ready to be filled in. Nan Pierce, with quiet gentle footsteps, shuttled her way between us and their lean-to kitchen. She served up her trademark rice pudding with a nutmeg-encrusted skin on top, so thick you might just bounce a penny off it, and which she broke with a spoon to reveal the creamy steaming pudding beneath.

'Homemade.' Dad Pierce would say, 'No one makes rice pudding like my Mary.'

He was the only one that didn't know it was Ambrosia rice pudding out of a tin, the skin on top engineered by Mary by placing the pudding under the grill. He never did find out.

We children piled onto the settee as Blackie, my grandparents' Scots terrier, fussed and shuffled on his short legs, his asthmatic wheezing growing steadily worse as we teased him. We would half listen to the grown-ups talk of the old days in Pwllheli and Dolwyddelan, of relatives in Canada and New York living glamorous lives, and of failing health, of which there was little evidence. Blackie would begin to scratch incessantly, and Nan Pierce would reassure us in her gentle voice and north Wales accent:

'Don't worry, it's not fleas. It's just that his blood's too rich.'

When it was time to leave we would crane our necks and wave goodbye from the street at the bottom of the steps, and from his vantage point above my grandfather would wave back and raise his gaunt and bushy-browed face to look around, all disapproving of the industrial view and the smoky air. Like one of the Old Testament prophets from my Sunday school stories he stood on this man-made crag of a southern hill, breathing the unclean atmosphere and surveying the colliery's sprawling mass below, having long since weighed this place in the balance, and found it wanting. Then he turned to go back inside, his expression showing his pained acceptance of the wrongness of it all.

And so to Crescent Street, to see my Nana and Dada, my father's parents. Their street, Crescent Street, was built right on the eastern bank of the Taff. It was a double terrace, and George and Lily, together with my Uncle Wyndham, their youngest son, lived at number 19 which, like the other houses on this side of the street had a long garden separated from the river by a flood wall that would prove to be, ultimately, useless as to its intended purpose. The wall had a flat top which was wide enough to run along for almost the whole length of the street. On the other side of the wall was a broad stretch of pebbles which we called the Riverstones. All this was enclosed since the only way to reach the Riverstones and the river itself was to pass through one of the houses on this particular side of the street, get to the bottom of the garden and jump up over the flood wall. On the far side of the river the bank was so steep and craggy that it had prevented the clearance of a small patch of the original ancient woodland that had once covered the whole of the South Wales Valleys. The Riverstones was a place half in and half out of the world of people, houses and streets, the liminal river wall separating my grandfather's carefully tended vegetable garden from a glimpse of the wildwood, of this place as it was before industry, before coal. This was a place made in answer to childhood's wants, a semi-private adventure playground of trees and water and chuckable stones where you could play out of sight of the grown-ups in the houses on the other side of the wall. Very soon I would be old enough to be allowed to explore that world beyond the wall. I contented myself, for now, with the house and garden as places to explore.

Today, the streets of our towns and villages, even those most agreeable, are not much more than rows of houses, each front door a barrier, a permanent and respected boundary between public and private worlds. But then, and these were the last of such times, streets worked differently. They were places for living, extensions of the home and, if weather permitted, most doors were likely to be open. The barrier between public street and private home was permeable and diffuse. Our streets then were places for talking, strolling, greeting and consoling, for gossip, debate and argument and children's play.

No street that I ever knew had such a vibrancy of life as did Crescent Street. Capped by the Rechabite Coffee Tavern and Flower's grocery shop at one end, and the cul-de-sac of Taff Street at the other, it traced three hundred yards of all that was most vital about our valleys. Children constantly hurtled along it, ducking in and out of each other's houses, scraping knees and laughing. Miners off-shift sparked their Segs shoe studs off its kerbstones and spat with the accuracy of marksmen into its gutters. On Summer evenings, wives and mothers would bring their kitchen chairs out onto the pavement and sit with their knitting, waiting like knowing spiders in their webs, to seize company and gossip as it passed by.

The women accepted guardianship in particular of the strip of pavement running along the frontage of their home by keeping it spotless with a dedication we might find puzzling today. At number 19, my grandmother would ensure that this line of public sandstone flags advertised to all the private propriety, order and cleanliness of the home on the other side of the well-scrubbed doorstep. Brushed, disinfected and rinsed day by day, that four yard strip of public stones in private stewardship was a flag raised on that tiny 'tidy' territory; it was a staked claim to respectability and to a right to connect with the community beyond. The right to keep open one's front door was so earned.

When my grandmother wasn't scrubbing it, I would use that strip of pavement to practise my skill at marbles. On my hands and knees, my cheek pressed hard against the stone, I'd squint through one eye, planning each shot, carefully taking into account every bump and contour of the stone. With total concentration I would practise for hours, the stone's surface becoming a familiar miniature landscape that I alone could navigate with mastery, knowing its tiny quirks as no one else could hope to do. In this way I planned my advantage if I should be challenged to a game of 'keepsies', since I would be the general who had chosen his ground. I kept my 'alleys' and 'bompers' in an old tin that had once held chocolate brazils. There was a fair amount of winning and losing over time, but I always held back my favourite 'alley', with its navy blue swirl in its centre and a tiny dent in its surface that only I would ever notice. That one was special, for practise only, and never to be risked.

My father's mother, Lilian Margaret Williams, was born in 1909 ('nineteen-ought-nine', as she always put it) in Moy Road, Aberfan. At the age of fourteen she was sent away to work 'in service'. She ended up in Eastbourne as a maid-of-all-work to a family of 'broken down toffs' as she recalled them. She hated it, of course, and the pain of her homesickness echoed down the decades whenever she retold the story.

'They think we Welsh live in caves,' she would say, 'but that dirty bugger (the head of the Eastbourne household) would spit on the grate like a navvy. *Ych a Fi.*' It took me some years to realise that cleaning that grate would have been one of her duties.

I can picture her clearly now, sitting up in bed, as she was wont to do on cold winter evenings, wearing a cardigan and a furry green hat reserved only for this purpose. Her dentures out, and sucking on a Minto, she'd read the *News Of The World*, a copy of which would last her all week, muttering under her breath, 'Well, well, well, the dirty buggers.' The piercing of any hypocrisy of those in public life seemed always to bring her satisfaction.

She would always steadfastly refuse to relate to me the stories of defrocked vicars or politicians caught in scandal from the pages of the paper, since I was too young to know about such things.

'Never you mind,' she'd say.

At such times she'd relate to me stories of her own past. Of how, when she was a girl growing up in Moy Road, swarms of 'black pats' (cockroaches) lived in daytime behind the wallpaper, gnawing away at the flour and water paste used to hang it, and how at night they would swarm out and carpet the floor under cover of darkness, so that if you needed the chamber pot in the night you would have to crunch them underfoot. Of the one occasion she'd gone underground, when for some reason they'd allowed wives down the pit to take a look, that it was alive with black pats down there too, but the rats were even worse. Of how she'd seen the coalface where her husband worked; eighteen inches high and six inches of water in it.

'You work hard now at school, so you can wear a shirt and tie to work every day,' she told me.

She swore the weather was different when she was young; the summers hotter, and that in one particular year, even at the Easter holiday, you could have fried an egg on the pavement.

Many times she told me of the occasion she nearly died of quinsy, and the doctor was called. He lanced the abscess and gave her an emetic of hot vinegar so that she vomited up the foulness of it.

And she told me that she had not a single tooth in her head because her parents had paid for a dentist to extract them all in one sitting, and that that had been her eighteenth birthday present from them. In those days that was seen as a mercy and an economy, since the assumption was that one would lose all one's teeth in any case, and it was better to get the whole thing over and done with.

Half remembered fragments of her childhood. If I'd known the right questions to ask, I could have learned so much more. Still, such as these memories are, I do not want them to die.

Other than that time away in Eastbourne, Lily moved only once in her life; when she married George Lewis from Taff Street and they settled here at number 19. In their youth they had known that generation who were the beginning of this place. Her father had spoken no English and had moved here from Machynlleth for a job in the pit, while her husband, George, had sprung from a confusion of Irish and Pembrokeshire antecedents, all, Welsh and Irish, arriving here for the same reason. They raised three surviving children in number 19: the eldest, my Aunty Eileen, my father David next, and then my Uncle Wyndham. She was from Welsh Presbyterian stock and he from Irish Catholic, but by the time I was born they practised no religion. Lily had become convinced that chapel piety was too often hypocritical and

George had broken with Rome by the more direct means of laying out the local priest with a single punch when he had raised a hand to Wyndham, then an altar boy.

They had lived through the General Strike, world war, lockouts and times of semi-starvation, when men had spirited sheep from the mountainside to slaughter surreptitiously for food. George as a young miner had been blacklisted for (in the management's eyes at least) having led a walkout strike from the pit. He had been working as an overman, responsible for the quota of coal set for his team of men. They had been joined by a lad of fourteen who was slightly built and simply wasn't yet capable of the bruising physical demands of the shift. The quota was not met. My grandfather was warned to get the young boy in line or pay would be docked. His reply was to ask the manager: 'Would it help if I put a ball and chain on the poor little bastard?' His reward was to be sacked on the spot.

As he left the colliery, hundreds of men, the entire shift, walked out with him. They followed him back to Crescent Street and the crowd gathered in the street outside number 19 discussing what to do next. George knew that his days as a miner in any pit were now over and not wishing this on anyone else he leaned out of the upstairs window, and into an expectant hush, he made his first and last political speech: 'Go back to work, you daft bastards!' he said. And so they did.

Afterwards came unemployment and a resort to pleading to 'the Parish', then work as a lamplighter, trudging along the darkening streets from street light to street light, a ladder over his shoulder. Later he worked as a stoker in the gasworks in Merthyr. My father as a child had once watched him work there as he shovelled coal into the maw of the furnace which opened and closed mechanically in an unending cycle.

'I saw a man being controlled by a machine, when it ought to be the other way round,' my father told me. 'Mind you,' he said, 'that's why your Dada has arms like Popeye.'

By the time I came along, Dada had moved on to clean work on the production line at the enormous Hoover factory in Pentrebach, which he would continue until retirement. My father would follow him there, but as an apprentice and then a production engineer, thanks to the secondary education he had enjoyed, but which was denied his own father. Of all the good things of the earth that were withheld from those generations – decent housing, clothes and food, medicine, warmth and comfort – the thing most malign was the denial of the chance to learn. This was the greatest cruelty.

Outside of work, my grandfather was always busy. 'Jack of all trades, master of none', my grandmother used to say. His garden was his chief concern but he could manage basic carpentry and bricklaying, he could glaze a window, paint and decorate and even cobble shoes on an iron last he kept in his shed. I recall him mixing cement with my father to build our lean-to bathroom, shifting the heavy mixture with seeming ease, handling the shovel methodically with his big blue veined hands. The only jobs he steered clear of were those involving the innards of machinery or of electrical wiring, which was just as well as the village had quite enough amateur electricians, men whose expertise was gleaned from a partial understanding of the industrial electrics of the pit, but who were nonetheless enthusiastic to 'have a go' at domestic wiring.

Though he very rarely talked politics, my grandfather laid the blame for past misfortunes squarely at the door of the Tory Party.

'They'd chain you to the workbench if they could,' he said.

Even so, as evidence of the durability of working class

Conservatism nearly every Valleys community could at that time boast a 'Con' club (the word 'Constitutional' often standing in euphemistically for 'Conservative'). Ours was the Gordon Lennox Club in Nixonville, named after a Tory Party election agent of the nineteenth century. It was a great red-brick-and-stone built building with several bars, a dance hall and a snooker room. It even had a balcony over the street on the first floor, constructed, I cannot help but suppose, for the use of any Tory candidate that might be courageous enough to make a speech from it. As far as I am aware, none ever did. 'The Gordons', as we called it, lay directly on the route home to Cottrell Street from my grandparents' house in Crescent Street. In later years my grandfather would often walk me along Nixonville, holding my hand, taking me home after a day at school followed by tea at number 19. Strangely, when we got to that part of the street he always guided me to the other side of the road and we would literally 'pass by on the other side' of The Gordons, walking past the pithead baths, opposite, instead. He never explained why he did this and in my childish acceptance of things I never asked him. Looking back in adulthood I realised that he would not even walk on the pavement outside a con club, let alone enter one.

I loved those short walks with my grandfather, usually my only time alone with him. We'd walk along hand in hand, me chattering incessantly and asking the kind of questions children ask in a never ending stream, him taciturn and full of forbearance. He was a thin wiry man, but with those powerful hands and arms that come as a legacy of a life spent shovelling coal. At this point in his life he was beginning to stoop just a little, and he breathed heavily after we had been walking even a short way, his lungs having been damaged by coal dust. One winter, as the days grew shorter, he bought me a little battery-powered 'Pifco' torch from Woolworth's in Merthyr so I could light our way in the gathering dark. It was a prized possession of mine, and I carefully illuminated our footsteps as we passed the 'Daggers', the local ex-servicemen's club, its doors swinging open as the first regulars went in, wafting the warm beery air of the interior into our faces as we passed. I loved the idea of this little handheld instrument cutting through the dark at my command. It was even better when it was raining, when I could light up the needle-like streaks of raindrops caught in its beam. I remember once asking him: 'Dada, when it's raining, would you get wetter if you ran through it, or if you walked?'

'Well if you walked, I suppose, because you'd be out in the wet for longer,' he said.

'But if you ran, wouldn't you hit loads of raindrops that you would have missed if you'd been moving slower?' I asked. He snorted. I kept on puzzling about this out loud and at length all the way along Nixonville as we meticulously avoided The Gordons, and over the bridge to home, which we reached safe and sound thanks to my conscientious work with the precious torch.

Each day my grandmother fought a meticulously planned battle with dirt and disorder in her home, her generalship both competent and committed. When she had taken care of the doorstep and the pavement 'out the front' she would move on indoors to command a creeping barrage on the carpets using her new wonder weapon, the upright Hoover. She viewed this roaring beast, as heavy as cast iron and smelling of dust and overheated rubber, with a mixture of respect and suspicion. The evidence was there that it worked when its dust bag was emptied, but she would follow up all the same, just to make sure, by scrubbing with a carpet brush and a damp cloth, like a choleric old colonel caught up in the age of the machine gun, who still believed in the ultimate power of the bayonet.

Windows were attacked with bubble-gum-pink Windolene and rags made from old vests that she drew from the pockets of her pinny. The furniture, heavy and brown and top quality, having been bought at Schwartz's in Merthyr, was assaulted with Pledge. The outside toilet in the garden was mopped up with bleach and hot water heated on the kitchen stove, and her sink, the kitchen 'bosh', was beaten into submission with lashings of Vim.

Even the front room, which the family never used as it was kept 'for best', was scrubbed, hoovered and polished until the woodwork gleamed and the scent of lavender filled the air.

Wash day followed a different battle plan involving the conscription of hot tub and mangle, bags of Reckitt's Blue, a packet of Omo, and pale yellow bricks of Sunlight soap for rubbing on shirt collars. Wearing her pinny with tiny blue flowers on it, her pockets full of clothes pegs, her hands plunged in water so hot that I would never be able to bear it, she worked amidst the steam rising from the pans of vests and shirts simmering on the stove. In my mind's eye I can walk toward her now, amidst a smell of hot clean cotton and billowing steam, and see her clearly with her fine white hair, her hands raw and red from the near boiling soapy water, the translucent skin about her pale blue eyes creasing as she smiles at me.

'Let me peg these out a minute,' she'd say, 'and then we'll have a proper cup of tea.'

Of all the Sunday visits to Crescent Street, summer Sundays were my best beloved. Summer saw my grandfather's garden at its abundant best, whirring and buzzing with insects and radiating warmth from its black alluvial soil. Nearest to the lean-to kitchen with its tar paper roof that blistered in hot sunshine were planted the salad vegetables. Tidy rows of lettuce, beetroot, radishes and spring onions which released their keen aroma after rain. Next to them was a small patch of used tea leaves and eggshells which my grandfather allowed to rot down to compost, convinced that these two odd ingredients made the best fertiliser of all. Just here, somewhere under the path, was an ants' nest. The ants would emerge through cracks in the concrete in thin lines of march. Normally we ignored them, but if any turned up in the kitchen I would be tasked to pour boiling water from the kettle onto the cracks in an attempt to kill off the nest. The hot water hissed and crackled its deadly way through the little fissures in the path, seemingly destroying all it flooded, but it never worked and the ants just kept on marching.

Next came the rows of onions swelling in the earth, the lacy fronds of carrot leaves and pea sticks laden with pods. Then cabbages, under constant attack from caterpillars and slugs. Often my grandfather would ask me to help deal with these pests, and I would scan the undersides of the cabbage leaves looking for the little green caterpillars, dispatching them by smearing their fat bodies with my thumb. The slugs I flipped up with a garden cane onto the path before dousing them with salt, watching them roil in a chemical burn – the watching of it both compulsive and repulsive at the same time. When bored with this, I would go after the cabbage white butterflies that laid their eggs on the cabbage leaves. I fenced and swiped at them with the cane, and on the rare occasions when I managed to hit one, their dusty wings would shatter and then be blown away like scraps of tissue paper in the breeze.

Beyond the cabbages were two long rows of runner beans with peach-fuzz pods that snapped with a satisfying crack, trained on sticks seven feet tall. Next to my grandfather's brick-built shed was a shady patch of ground reserved for rhubarb, where it thrived and grew leaves wider than my outstretched arms. At the bottom of the garden, nearest the river, banked rows of potatoes would provide enough crop to last right through the autumn, and part of winter too.

But best of all were the redcurrant and blackcurrant bushes, close by the fence separating Dada's garden from Martha Annie's next door. Intended for baking tarts, these red and black drops of crystalline brightness were so juicy and tempting that we grandchildren ensured they rarely made it as far as the kitchen. Today, no fruit I taste matches the deliciousness of those berries from long ago, when my seven-year-old taste buds had not yet atrophied.

There were many gardens and allotments like this in the two villages, all made with great effort and often from some necessity. Expertise was shared by word of mouth; I recall no gardening books or magazines being read. Havens of autonomy, they were the domain almost exclusively of men; here, in complete contrast to their experience of the world of work they were free to create for themselves order and excellence and beauty. Most grew vegetables, but flowers had their devotees, too, and some would compete in local shows, striving for perfection. Mr Jones at number 5 in our street grew chrysanthemums for competition; flawless orbs of colour. He engineered their perfect symmetry by timing to the minute their exposure to the sun by means of paper bags tied around the blooms. Others worked with animals; Tom Cornwall at number 3 bred rabbits for his Sunday dinner; at number 4, Penry

Clements bred and raced pigeons. There was at least one pigeon loft in every street in those days. Penry's loft was amongst the biggest, made of offcuts of wood hammered together, and almost as high as his house. My Uncle Wyndham once took me to see the homemade aviary of a friend of his, and I walked through a nondescript shed door into an eruption of exotic birdsong; tropical plumage flashing in fifty different colours as the tiny birds whirled about my head and perched on my hands. These gardens were places where the greyness of the world could be driven out and where, through careful guardianship, better worlds could be made in miniature.

On those summer Sundays my grandfather's garden would provide us with our tea: hot boiled potatoes smothered with salty Carmarthenshire butter, with tinned salmon and spring onions soused in peppered vinegar. Co-op Indian Prince tea brewed strong and drunk with heaped teaspoons of sugar, and rhubarb tart and Ideal milk for desert. Crammed into the tiny kitchen, the adults would trade gossip and tease us children and each other. My Nana would tut at my grandfather's habit of drinking his tea from the saucer, as he blew at it to cool it down. Uncle Wyndham might sing Elvis numbers into a spoon, my Aunty Eileen saying, ''Ark at him, b'there,' and rolling her eyes in exasperation. I might take up station sitting cross-legged under the kitchen table, listening to the adults' talk and laughter and understanding only half of it. The warmth of summer air would drift in from the open back door, as I was slyly fed bits of cooked ham before time by my grandmother, and I would feel wholly at home and happy.

I recall on one of these summer Sunday afternoons climbing onto the roof of the coal *cwtch* my grandfather had built from corrugated iron, and lying flat on my back to stare at the stillness of a sky of silent blue. The sun was gently warm on my face and the smell of the garden, damp from recent watering, drifted around me, and quite suddenly I felt a deep, untroubled peace. In that peace was a child's certainty of the permanence of things. The future was far off and indistinct and it was ludicrous to contemplate it. Time slept. This place, this garden, this safe harbour that my grandfather had made would always be and these times would never end. Live placidly, like this, and all these things would be true. Happiness was real and unending, and I was immortal.

Then, as I lay there something profound happened to me. I remember it with perfect clarity some forty-five years later. Indeed, I have no doubt that it is in fact the reason I remember the whole episode of clambering up onto that shed roof and lying flat to look at the sky. For a few moments, something in the way I was perceiving the world was suddenly shifted. I still saw the blue above me, still felt the sun on my face, still heard the buzz of insects in the garden, but now there was more. Whatever barrier, membrane or veil that there was, beforehand, between me and my senses and what was in the world around me – sky, shed, garden, sounds, and sunlight, whatever that barrier is that marks us off as beings from the wider world – was, well, gone. Just for a few moments, although it may as well have lasted a day, or a decade, because the impact of it is with me still and will never leave me. Just for those few moments there was no sky or shed or garden or anything else in the wide world that was separate from me. All these things, myself included, were now one thing, one being. I floated, for those moments, as a part of everything, no longer apart, but a part.

This was not an emotion. Although I felt content and

peaceful, this changed perception of things was not, of itself, contentment or peace. It surrounded those feelings. It contained them. As it contained me. As it contained everything.

Seconds later this shift in the world was gone and things were back as they had been; myself and the world apart, with only my senses to show me the world that lay beyond my skin.

This change in all the ways of perceiving, this subsuming of self into the world, I know now to have happened to many other people, at times all through history and in all parts of the world. Some might explain what happened to me that day as some kind of spiritual experience, the kind of experience that some people with a mystical religious view might actively seek out through meditation, or prayer or even fasting. But I was not praying, I had no concept of what meditation was, and any thought of fasting would have been regarded, by that small boy on the shed roof, with horror. I was simply a child, being happy, and it happened to me. I did not wish for it. I did not understand it. I did not think of God. Afterwards I was not worried or disturbed and perhaps I thought this sort of thing happened to everyone from time to time. I did not have the capacity, the vocabulary even, to talk to anyone about it, and I have not ever spoken of it until now, until I put down here the words I can best muster to describe what happened that day.

I sometimes wonder, if the small boy I was that day were somehow to talk to me as I am now, a man in my fifties, and ask me what I thought had happened, then what would I say? After all my schooling and studying and all my experience of life and all the many people that I have learned from, and all the hundreds of books I have read in all those years, what would I tell him?

I would have to tell him that I knew no more than he did about what had happened and what it meant, or if it meant anything at all. But I could tell him that this momentary change in how the world was, and how he was in the world, would happen just one more time, while he was still a boy, and never again after that. I would tell him that this second episode would, I think, teach him something. And I would tell him not to worry, not to be fearful. But that last part he would know, in any case.

I climbed down off the shed roof and planted my feet on the solid ground of the concrete garden path. I strolled slowly back to the back kitchen of the house in the warm air of that late summer afternoon and I could hear my Uncle Wyndham washing the dishes and humming along to *Sing Something Simple* on the transistor radio. And I was wholly content.

I was a happy child. Even so, around this time, when I must have been six or seven years old, I dreamed, for the first time, a nightmare that would revisit me several times, and would lodge itself vividly in my memory. In the dream I stood at twilight at the entrance to a rutted and uneven roadway made of muddy black earth. The entrance was flanked by gateposts on each side; twin stone gargoyles with owl-like, malign, expectant eyes that watched me closely. They were still, dumb, stone but they were waiting for me, I knew, to step forward, and walk along the road. They wanted me to step forward. They wordlessly demanded it. There was no way around the gateposts because to each side there were black, thorny trees packed so close together as to be impenetrable, their branches trailing to the ground like coils of barbed wire. I knew that just a handful of steps would have me committed to the muddy road. I knew that if I did set off, I'd feel relieved, the decision made. But the road beyond this open gateway was dark and I could not see where it led and I was transfixed by fear of it, and of the faces on the gateposts too. I somehow knew that if I passed beyond the gargoyles, there was no changing my mind; I would have to carry on along the black road wherever it took me.

In an agony of indecision, I hesitated. I thought I should be more brave, because I knew many others had already taken the road – it was churned up by the feet of hundreds of travellers that had come this way before me – and yet my fear of the ghoulish stone faces, and my knowledge that there was no reversing that journey kept me rooted to the spot. I was ashamed of my fear. And so for a long time the shame and the fear fought inside me demanding a decision, and the gargoyles watched with a terrifying disapproval, and I thought they scorned my cowardice, but still I would not move. Finally I woke, relieved, but also full of guilt because my fear had been stronger than my shame.

# School Days and Wine Gums

By the time I was old enough to attend, a new school had been built to replace the one destroyed. Ironically, the new Ynysowen Primary was constructed right on top of a slag heap, the oldest in the village said my grandfather, and needed specially designed foundations and walls that would flex with the undependable earth beneath. Some years later, after I had left for secondary school, the coal waste beneath Ynysowen would spontaneously combust, deep underground; it took upwards of a year, much drilling and thousands of gallons of water pumped at pressure beneath the surface in order to make it safe. In the meanwhile children attended lessons along taped-out paths, tendrils of smoke rising from the playing fields on either side of them.

For me, though, the school was a revelation. Everything about it was brand new. Having benefited from donations from individuals and organisations around the world as contributions to the Disaster Fund, the brand new building, still smelling of fresh paint, was packed with never-before-used toys, games, sports equipment, books, poster paint, crayons, pencils, and wonder of wonders – felt-tipped pens.

On my very first day at school I had Ready Brek for breakfast, with the top-of-the-milk stirred in and enough sugar on top to form a semi-dissolved translucent crust floating on the steamy surface. We set out and Allyson ran ahead with her friends to the junior section of the school whilst Mam walked me to the infants. The route to school, most wonderfully, involved walking right past Terry Martin's shop.

Terry's was a newsagent-cum-sweetshop. We walked in and were enfolded by its all-pervasive smell of sweet fruity sugar, newsprint and clove; Terry himself favoured clove mints, just like my grandfather who demolished them by the half pound since he'd given up smoking. Just one small room, the wall shelves, counter, and even the floor were crammed with ranks of jars of boiled sweets and other treats even more exotic. Sherbet Lemons jostled for shelf space with multi-coloured Pear Drops with their acid bite, and they in turn with Gobstoppers as big as our fists, Rhubarb and Custard, American Hard Gums, Dolly Mixtures, Cherry Lips, Sour Grape chewing gums that had you spitting purple, Bonbons dusted white or yellow, Flying Saucers, and jars of sherbet in a half dozen vivid colours. The counter groaned under the weight of its boxes of Black Jacks, Fruit Salads, Sherbet Fountains, Sweet Cigarettes, and Spanish Gold Sweet Tobacco. There were 'Bazooka Joe' chewing gums that you should never ever swallow, grown-ups said, lest the gum loop around your appendix and make it burst. Alongside were Love Hearts, Fizzers, and Parma Violets (whose perfumed taste made me gag), Treets, tubes of Smarties, and packets of Spangles, brittle like coloured glass. A large toffee tray sat there with its miniature hammer, alongside the Milky Bars, Revels, Bar Sixes, Aeros and Toffos, Tooty Frooties, Turkish Delight, and Drumsticks. And so I stood there, entranced, paralysed and struck dumb by this cornucopia of choice.

Terry Martin himself presided over this tiny space as if it

were designed for much more than mere commerce; it was, too, a place to linger with a customer for the sake of gossip, and as far as we children were concerned, a performance space also.

'Well now, Mrs Lewis, good to see you. And this must be your oldest boy?' He extended his hand to me. Mam nudged me gently, so I shook hands, mortified. It was the first time I had ever shaken hands with anyone.

'So now then, first day at school?' he asked. I nodded.

'Well, I can see why you're being careful. A big important choice to make – the right sweets for the first day at school. Now don't you worry, I can help!' and he crouched down to my eye level. 'Something small you want, see?' he said, winking at Mam. 'So it fits in your pocket and the teacher won't see. And something quiet, no rustly wrappers, so the teacher won't hear. And something you can share, if you meet a new butty.'

Terry then stood, took a deep breath and, with heartfelt conviction as if he were a consultant surgeon recommending the best course of action for a needy patient, he said: 'Mrs Lewis, I would say, for this young man, two ounces of wine gums will do the job.'

'That alright then?' Mam asked me, smiling. I nodded, having only a hazy idea of what wine gums actually were. At the same time, the certainty of the grown-ups about this prescription was something I did not feel I could gainsay. And so the sweets were weighed and dispensed into a small paper bag and handed to me. I peeped inside to see the fruity coloured shapes with their strong citrusy smell, and I squeezed the softly yielding geometry of one of them between thumb and forefinger. It didn't occur to me to try one then and there and so I shoved the bag into the pocket of my scratchy grey shorts to investigate later. I soon forgot they were there, and didn't eat them at school after all.

My mother thanked Terry and we turned to leave, but just as we opened the door with its 'ping!' of a bell, Terry called after us. ''old on, 'old on, I nearly forgot!' he said. 'Today's special offer! Free Swiss watch for everyone on their first day at school.' He then fumbled in a box behind the counter and produced a toy wristwatch. It was shiny blue plastic with a navy wristband. Terry crouched down beside me again.

'What's the time by you, Mrs Lewis?' he asked.

'Ten to, Terry,' Mam said.

Then with great deliberation he adjusted the hands of the watch. He held it to his ear and said: 'There we are, ticking lovely now, it is.' And he fastened it on my wrist. 'Very good, very good,' said Terry. 'Now you'll never be late for school.' He beamed.

'Say 'thank you, Mr Martin',' my mother said. So I did.

As we left the shop I felt ten feet tall. I had a watch. Just like my father did. I think I realised it was just a toy, and it didn't really tick, but that didn't bother me at all. It looked dead swanky on my wrist, and I kept looking at it all the way to school.

Terry knew how to win a customer. For years afterwards, I would go out of my way to buy my sweets from Terry Martin. To this day I have a wine gum habit that is tough to break. I also bought my comics in his shop and soon became addicted to them too. I started off with the *Dandy* and Korky the Cat, or else *Topper* with Mickey the Monkey before graduating to *Victor,* 'the famous action paper for boys', with its working class hero Alf Tupper (The Tough of the Track), an athlete who won out against posh boy opposition on the running track week after week, fuelled solely by a diet of fish and chips. Terry even occasionally stocked American comics, like *Marvel* and *DC*. I enjoyed the Superman and Spiderman stories, but what really captured my imagination were the small ads for toys which these American publications contained, and which were as impossibly exotic as they were unobtainable. For some weeks I lusted after a 'Polaris Nuclear Sub' that was advertised as 'seven feet long and big enough for 2 kids', and which featured missiles and torpedoes that really fired as well as a 'real working periscope'. I could not believe that such a thing was real. I returned to read the advert again and again and memorised its every word even though I knew this was nothing more than a pipe dream. It was priced in dollars and cents, and no one I knew had any American money.

That first day at school, Mam and I, with new watch on my wrist, left Terry's shop and walked past Noel Terrace with a steady stream of other mothers trailing little ones and the bigger kids running and swerving to overtake. Just after the end of the row of houses, the view opened up so that we could look down on the pit yard. A distant metallic clanking sounded out and a steam engine puffed white clouds into the cool September air.

I cannot remember taking leave of my mother on that first day at school. I don't think there were tears (at least not from me). Now I am a parent myself, I see things as they must have been through her eyes. I see vividly, the first occasion when I dropped my eldest son off at nursery school thirty-odd years later. I remember he looked unsure and a little sad as I waved goodbye to him.

'He'll be alright, best you go,' the teacher had said to me,

then would we be allowed to ask our class teacher's permission. If that was given, we would then have to wash our hands before handling any of the books. To read a book we had to stand opposite its place on the bookshelf and read it standing there without moving – we were not allowed to sit, let alone take the book away with us. When finished, we had to place the book straight back onto the shelf and return to our classroom. Only one book was to be read per session. The first time I made it to the bookcases, alone in the school hall, I chose a Dr. Seuss book, *Green Eggs and Ham*. I liked the cover. I did not like the story. I didn't understand its humour and its rhyming form annoyed me. As I read I became tearful because I realised I could not choose another book to replace it. The rule was one book per session. It might be days or weeks, even, before I got another chance.

My adult self cannot fathom why any school would want to ration children's exposure to books in this way. I can only imagine that our predecessor school had some tremendous shortage, and the headteacher had become neurotic about keeping what books she had in good condition, so eking out their useful lifespan. In any case, I would sit in each assembly in the school hall, surrounded by the tempting covers all around me, feeling like a child in a sweet shop with not a penny to spend. How I yearned for those books. When I left, eventually, to move up to the junior school next door, I had managed to read only a handful.

The official opening day of the infant and junior schools happened in 1968. My teacher, Mrs Williams, who had daringly short hair and seemed so young and modern compared to some of the other teachers, briefed us that there would be 'important visitors' coming to see us and a plaque would be unveiled in the junior school next door. When the day came we were told to play quietly, and I immediately latched onto a box of brand new building blocks that I had lusted over for some time. They smelled strongly of new plastic and were multi-coloured and transparent so that if you looked through them the world turned bright yellow, or purple or deepest red, the colours having that almost edible vividness that we can only see in childhood. I had them all to myself and I began to build, with complete absorption, a complicated castellated tower with ramparts and stairways to its battlements. I was lost in my imagination when a small somewhat elderly man in a raincoat suddenly appeared, standing over me and smiling.

'Now that's impressive,' he said and he gestured at my creation with an unlit pipe that smelled faintly of cold, wet tobacco. 'What will you do next?' I was annoyed at this interruption, my building work had been so involving. I said, curtly: 'I'll build reinforcements.' It was a word I'd heard my father use.

He seemed satisfied and chuckled and moved on; a crowd of grown-ups in overcoats and shiny black shoes following him at a measured distance. Three or four men with cameras blazed away with flashbulbs. My concentration had been ruined, as I realised only a good deal of time later, by the 'important visitor' himself – the man who was there to unveil the plaque. It was Harold Wilson, Prime Minister of Great Britain and Northern Ireland.

That autumn I dreamed more than once of my walk to school being transfigured into nightmare. Just as I reached the end of the street of houses beyond Terry Martin's shop I looked down on the pit yard and, for a heartbeat, all was as it should be.

Then suddenly there was a great convulsion of the earth, and the once solid ground beneath my feet began heaving and swelling like the sea. The towers of the pithead winding gear and the great wheels, still turning, lurched from side to side. There was a hollow booming sound, from deep below the colliery yard, a low rumbling snarl of anger that vibrated the ground. Then there was a great jolting collapse of earth and stone and shrieking metal as a tear appeared in the ground between the towers, widening at startling speed until the towers themselves, though resisting, slowly folded and fell, swallowed by a now enormous sink hole in the valley floor. I felt the ground shudder and shift through the soles of my shoes. I was immobilised by fear. My throat constricted and my breathing came in rapid, shallow little gulps. As I watched, unable to look away, enormous gouts of flame then shot skyward out of the wound in the world that the pit had made, now growing wider still as more and more of the once solid and substantial buildings, railway tracks and roadways about its edges were swallowed by this great maw. The ground was slipping toward it, like sand in an hourglass, falling into flame. All that had been fixed was now in motion; whole streets, the whole village, the mountains either side, my whole childhood world, slipping and shuddering and being dragged into this abyss of fire, its edge moving inexorably closer to the spot where I stood. I knew I was going to die. It was the first time I had envisaged my own death, I think, and the fear of death overwhelmed me with a suffocating weight.

At this point I woke in dread. A dread not just of death, but something else too: the fact that in my dream I was certain that the earth was moving with a purpose. It was consuming the surface world deliberately. Hunting us. The whole thing was an act of all-consuming revenge.

What could be more fearful than this: that the solid ground beneath your feet might not be solid at all, but alive and knowing and simply tolerating you and your kind until it decided enough was enough, and so hauled you down, swallowing your world? What if this were a living, wrathful earth, aggrieved and vengeful, its mind made up that you – humanity, your industry, your buildings, your wounding presence itself, was found to be no longer bearable? And inside this apocalyptic dread, a fearful, fearful question: who was to blame? Who, in the end, had right on their side? The people or the earth?

I was too young to have put this question into words exactly, I did not articulate it or try to think through an answer, but the question was there, inside me; a visceral reality, like a stone in my belly.

And yet the waking world was still there in the morning. Still functioning. Still solid-seeming. Although for a long while that dream hung about me, like a vibration in the air, and I doubted the seeming dependability of the world.

More schooldays came and went, and soon I was judged old enough to make my way there alone. About that time, my mother began to train as a nurse up in Merthyr, and so each day after school I now headed for Crescent Street and Nana and Dada's house at number 19 for my tea. Every day at home time there was a challenge to be met on the way there.

I soon discovered, by following the example of the older boys, that if you were super-quick out of class at the end of the school day and ran at 'full pelt' down the steep footpath from school and over the foot bridge that crossed the river you might, just might, make it to the second footbridge that straddled the level crossing at the top of Crescent Street in time to beat one of the steam trains hauling coal wagons out of the colliery. The aim then was to stand squarely, legs apart and arms outstretched, on the central span of the bridge as the engine passed underneath, and the driver sounded the engine's whistle in salute. The steps and central span of the bridge were made from old railway sleepers, and on the central span there were little gaps between each, about an inch wide. So, as the engine puffed beneath, a great cloud of steam and soot would whoosh its way through the gaps and engulf us as we laughed and howled and bounced in the midst of a warm man-made fog that obliterated the rest of the world, swirling about us for a few seconds before it faded like breath on a windowpane. As we danced and hopped about, the coal wagons would rumble beneath us, and the bridge would tremble. It was deemed a great achievement, to beat the train and catch the cloud.

Tucked beneath the steps of this bridge was a tiny brick-built hut with a tin roof, just big enough to hold a wonky chair that the watchman would sit in. It was his job to open and close the big steel gates of the level crossing when one of the coal trains was due to pass. On colder days he lit a brazier, and in the mornings he'd fry bacon on the blade of a shovel with just a stump of handle, balanced on top of the glowing coals. On the way to school the Merthyr Vale boys would try to scrounge a rasher or two, but I never heard of them succeeding.

Just next to the hut was Flower's shop, which was a general grocer's, but which also had a counter given over to sweets. After he retired, my grandfather would often wait at the top of the street, opposite the shop, for my brother and me to emerge at the end of the school day and there was, most days, a thruppenny bit for each of us to spend. I would clutch the reassuring heaviness of the coin tightly in my hand as I ran across the road to the shop. Flower's sold most of the sweets that Terry Martin did, but sometimes they also carried toy tattoo patches that came in little cellophane envelopes. These were a favourite of mine. I remember choosing a skull and crossbones design one day, etched out in black and inky blue. To get the tattoos to work you licked your forearm and applied the paper patch picture side down to the wet spit, pressing hard. For a good result, the trick was to leave the patch on your skin for as long as you could bear to wait. I peeled mine off as slowly and steadily as I could, to reveal the result, blurred around its edges like a bruise. It was fantastic.

As I was a little older by now and the map of my world was extending slowly at its margins, it was deemed okay for me to play unsupervised on the Crescent Street Riverstones after tea each day. The river wall that separated my grandfather's garden from this new playground was five feet high and three feet wide, easy to climb, and its smooth flat top was broad enough to belt along at top speed from almost one end of the street to the other.

To drop down onto the other side of the wall, onto the Riverstones, was to leap through a doorway into another world, one which seemed reserved for us kids, as adults rarely ventured there.

Simply a gently sloping pebble-and-rock-strewn bank on the inside of a bend in the River Taff, the Riverstones were a side effect of the diverting of the course of the river by Victorian engineers when the pit was originally sunk. Shaped like a crescent moon it was pinched off at each end by high walls and tangles of Japanese knotweed, brambles and 'policeman's helmet' plants with their exploding seed pods. Because of this it was accessible only through the houses and gardens of Crescent Street, and so just a few of us children had uninvited access there. The river was so polluted back then that it generally ran black and there was little that lived in it, save sometimes a few sticklebacks and tiny bullheads, nervous in the shallows and hard to find. In summer when the river ran low, the sole plant life beneath the water, a greenish algal slime, would find itself stranded above the surface and its decomposing stench would fill the air.

And yet this was my own wild place, to be explored over and over, a place where I could lose myself and never be bored no matter how much time I spent there. I made a friend of Bryan Griffiths, who lived at number 16 and was the same age as me. Bryan stood out from most of us with his fair hair and blue eyes. He laughed easily and was unfailingly kind, but I liked him most because he was clever. I liked to be around clever people. Together we would spend hours looking for the perfect stones for throwing. Flat ones for skipping, counting off the bounces in competition with each other. Sausage-shaped stones were for 'bombing', producing the perfect splashless 'thock' of an Olympic diver if you got good height, and the spin just so. Floating – and sinkable – targets were greatly prized and we would scour the riverbank searching for bombardable jetsam. Since the river was a place where many had no qualms about disposing of their rubbish, there was generally no shortage of fresh target material. Bottles were best of course. Thrown in as far upstream as we could manage, they floated through our furious barrage of splashing stones as we each raced to be the one to fire the fatal shot. Each pop bottle became a little vitreous Bismarck, a dangerous enemy battleship that had to be stopped at all costs before all was lost, as it made a break for the open water south of Taff Street where the great Victorian arches supporting the railway line marked the end of our territory. With so much at stake, each successful hit was greeted with howls of victory.

Bottles were best, yes, but tin cans would do and could be swamped by a near miss or struck full-on with a satisfying 'dink'. Failing that, cardboard boxes could be commandeered into the enemy fleet. They soaked up loads of damage before they sank, like battling old Dreadnoughts.

When all other options were exhausted, we'd make do with water borne branches and sticks, but that really was scraping the barrel – after all they were a bugger to hit and wouldn't sink at all.

On late summer afternoons we would switch targets. This was because, as the days of summer wore on, the river attracted great swarms of midges that drifted like clouds of smoke above the water. These midges, in turn, attracted the swifts. So dark as to appear almost black, the swifts were mute boomerang shapes of pure momentum. Blurred embodiments of speed, they darted and flicked along the line of the river, feeding on the wing. My *Book of British Birds*, bought for me by my grandmother from WHSmith's in Merthyr, told me that the common swift spent more time on the wing than any other bird in the world, and that they hunted, fed and drank and even slept in flight, touching down only to care for their chicks in their nests. They flew relentlessly, scores of them, banking sharply, up and down this narrow strip of water, between the Riverstones and the tiny remnant of the Wildwood on its leg-breakingly steep bank on the other shore, gobbling down thousands of midges between them whilst still in mid-air. They formed an aerobatic mass just above our heads, never seeming to tire, or to be in any way concerned by our human presence. Sometimes they flew so close to us that we could have reached out and touched them, if only they hadn't been moving so blindingly fast.

The whole set-up crystallised in my childish imagination as being exactly like the climactic scene of the movie *633 Squadron* – a favourite of mine which had thrilled me, as a squadron of De Havilland Mosquito bombers ran the gauntlet of furious Nazi ack-ack, constrained in their manoeuvrings by a narrow Norwegian Fjord, fighting their way to destroy a factory vital to the enemy war effort. All the while the aircrews knew that the chances of success and survival were slimmer than slim. (My grandparents had recently acquired a black and white TV with big clunking push buttons to change the channel, and this film became an immediate Sunday afternoon favourite of mine. I revelled in the movie's story of striving on against hopeless odds, like Horatius on the bridge, as I suppose most small boys do.) So, there we were, combatants in a narrow strip of airspace; the swifts as the Mosquito Squadron, and Bryan and I as the ack-ack crews. We put up a frenzied barrage of pebbles, thrown three at a time, straight into the aerial wizardry of the speeding birds. We learned that since the swifts were so fast, one had to aim just ahead of the target to have any chance of coming close. We must have launched tens of thousands of pebbles in all those summer evenings, and we carried on throwing until our arms and shoulders ached with effort and we were clammy with sweat, until we were finally defeated by the encroaching darkness. There were thrilling near misses as the birds swirled about our heads, showing no fear, jinking and turning on a sixpence. But though we must have launched ten thousand little stones at those birds over those summer evenings, and kept on trying three or four summers in a row, these swifts, who after all could catch a tiny insect in mid-air, had no trouble dodging our clumsy efforts. There was never a single casualty. And thank heaven for it, for I don't know what we would have done, save panic, if faced with a dead or dying bird.

Indeed, the pair of us were proved to be cowards the day we stumbled upon, whilst playing on the Riverstones, a bag of drowned puppies someone had hurled over the river wall by means of disposal. We stared, horrified, for a long time, not wanting to get too close but unable to look away. These were the first sentient things I had ever seen dead. Bryan grabbed a stick.

'Go on, you do it,' he said. 'Go on mun.'

'No chance,' I said. 'You.' Bryan used the stick to widen the opening of the bag so we could get a better view of the five or six little bodies, slick and wet. There was no rot, no stink of death. The puppies were as fresh to death as new-plucked daisies, the pale pink pads of their tiny paws held out on straight legs as if in supplication, bodies huddled together, as they might have been in life when crowding round their mother to feed. If they had been alive we would have picked one up and petted it. But as they were dead, neither of us had the courage to even prod them with that stick, though we desperately wanted to see it done. The shocking obscenity of death appearing like this, without warning, on an otherwise bright and normal day radiated out toward us, both nauseating and compelling. I could see Bryan was as disinclined as I was, every bit as timorous, when it came to poking the little corpses about. This surprised me, because his father was a miner after all, and everyone knew that miners were tough and not afraid of much, and I had assumed he would be too.

The next day, on arrangement, we ran straight back to the spot where the puppies had been, emboldened now, and full of a ghoulish greed to see more of what dead things looked and felt like. Perhaps this time we'd have the courage to prod them with a stick, or even nudge them with the toe of a shoe. But the puppies were gone. Thanks to the river rats which abounded there, most likely.

Our playtime on the Riverstones was ended each day by an adult shout calling us for tea at our respective houses, and I would scramble back into the garden of number 19. When I got to the house Nana would invariably throw up her arms in horror.

'*Ych a fi*! Look at the state of you!'

I'd be held firmly in her grip whilst being scrubbed with a fat yellow bar of Sunlight soap like a pat of butter, and a rough 'flannin' cloth. '*Djawled!* You'll catch a disease from that stinking river.' So I was thoroughly decontaminated over the old stoneware 'bosh' with hot water from the new gas geyser until my hands and face felt as if they were glowing.

The day of the dead puppies I sat down for a tea of Pek meat and waxy boiled potatoes coated with butter and Branston Pickle. As I ate, the bag of little bodies lingered in my thoughts. I did not mention it. It was not a thing to share with grown-ups. It would have been a grown-up, after all, who had done the deed. Grown-ups dealt with death – it was a concern of theirs and not of us kids. I thought they understood it. Hadn't I seen them deal with it? When a funeral happened in the street, they knew just what to do; the men wore black ties and their Sunday suits, and the women closed the curtains of each front room, blocking out the daylight. There was a hearse, and the minister came; Erastus Jones, perhaps, wearing his black homburg and carrying his bible, all stern propriety but with kind, tired eyes. As the cortege passed, the men in the street stopped what they were about, removed their caps and bowed their heads in silence. They knew just what to do; grown-ups always knew. Any one of them would have known what to do with a bag of drowned puppies, I thought.

Bryan and I had intruded, had stumbled upon, that glimpse of lifelessness and through that had glanced that aspect of the grown-up world that was most ugly and fearful. We had been interlopers there, just for a while, and I felt a little guilty about it. But sitting quietly afterwards in my grandparents' kitchen, having my tea, and no one any the wiser about what we had seen, I felt normality flooding back into my childhood world and I was glad to feel immortal once again.

# The Sound of Thunder

By the time I reached the age of seven or eight my horizons grew a little wider still; pretty much the whole of the village was mine to explore and I grew to know the streets and shops and *gwlis* intimately. I had moved a little further into the wider world. Often now, after school and on Saturdays, I would be sent on errands to the shops on Aberfan Road. Almost everything that a household needed could be bought in the village in those days.

The first 'self-service' shop had opened up in Merthyr and the adults talked about it, though I had yet to see it. Many voiced their suspicion of this new way of shopping and stressed to each other the importance of checking the numbers on the long till rolls handed to them at the checkout to search for mechanised swindles. 'It'll never catch on,' they said. So for my family, as yet, there was no 'weekly shop', and purchases were made day to day as the need arose.

My most common errand was to run to 'The Berni's' to buy twenty Player's Navy Cut for Dad. The Berni's was one of the legendary, now almost extinct, Italian cafés of the South Wales Valleys, which had been opened by Italian immigrants to the once booming coalfield. They had quickly grown to be beloved of Valleys people as they added a dash of continental style and sophistication to our high streets. Almost every Valleys town and village could boast of at least one Italian café. Merthyr had its Viazzani's, the Rhondda had its Bracchi's and Aberfan had the Berni's. Despite the name above the door it was run, confusingly, with cheerful efficiency and pride by a Mr and Mrs Emmanuelli. They spoke English perfectly, but with a heavy Italian accent. She would frequently switch to speaking Italian in order, so it seemed to me, to chide her husband for his constant over enthusiasm and off-colour jokes. This happened a lot.

The Berni's sold sweets and chocolates of course, but centre stage was given over to the enormous chrome and steel edifice of their coffee machine. It was polished to a mirror shine and towered over their high counter emitting gentle hissing sounds until called upon to make frothy coffee by whooshing a jet of pressurised steam, loud enough to drown out all conversation, into a jug of milk. A marvellous contraption, it could double up by means of a special attachment, as a cooker of 'steamed pies' – a distinctly Valleys delicacy – which would be flopped, soggy, hot and delicious, on to your plate; steaming away like a freshly wet nappy. The café also boasted a chest freezer with a sliding top that dispensed orange Jubblies in their odd triangular packs, as well as choc ices and lollies: Mivvies, Orange Maids, Funny Feet, Fabs and Funny Faces and, my favourite, Zoom Rocket lollies. Mr Emmanuelli also dispensed, from a fridge behind the counter, bricks of Sidoli ice cream, wedged between two wafers, with or without a chocolate flake. The whole place smelled of coffee and tobacco and hot milk. On damp and dismal days it was a pleasure to sit in the sheltering warmth of the café, sip at a cup of hot milk and peruse the colourful postcards pinned up on the sweetie shelves, with their pictures of sun-drenched Italian towns and seaside views, the Colosseum and the Leaning Tower of Pisa. I pictured my future self strolling through an Italian garden in the Mediterranean warmth, enjoying the shade of the cypress trees as the Valleys rain belted down outside.

If we had a Corona pop bottle to return to the café, my reward for fetching Dad's Player's Navy Cut was to spend the deposit due on the bottle on whatever I wanted. 'Please Return Bottle 3d', it said on the lids. This was enough for two ounces of loose sweets, extricated from one of the three long rows of sweetie jars arranged along the shelves on the back wall. I would agonise over the choice between boiled sweets (like Rhubarb and Custard) which were longer lasting, or Needler's Fruit Pastilles, which tasted better but had to be eked out by squashing them with my tongue to the roof of my mouth, letting them slowly dissolve whilst resisting the overwhelming urge to chew.

The Berni's was the place to find more upmarket confectionery too, like boxes of Black Magic or (All because the ladies love...) Milk Tray. Either of these were ideal choices for Mothers' Day. There were After Eights for Christmas as well as Matchmakers in mint or orange flavour, Fry's Chocolate Cream bars and Bourneville dark chocolate of which I was wary, unsure if I was allowed it since the TV advert said it was 'for adults only'.

The Berni's was a place to linger and adults gossiped as children gawped at the hundreds of sugary choices on offer. The Berni's seemed to me to be the beating heart of the village where everyone, in time, would meet everyone else.

Another frequent destination for errands was Trevor the Ironmonger's shop to fetch a pint of paraffin for the heater in our bathroom (Boom boom boom boom Esso Blue! sang the TV advert). Trevor was a small, neat man who wore a brown overall coat with carpenter's pencils in his top pocket. His shop, on the other hand, was anything but neat and he stood behind his counter surveying a welter of goods spread all around and so seemingly disorganised and topsy-turvy that it resembled the aftermath of an explosion. Shelves all around the walls were crammed, seemingly at random, with overflowing boxes of nails, screws, nuts and bolts of every conceivable size, sold singly or by the pound. Tins of paint and varnish, candles, chains, rope, piping and hand tools of every description filled even more boxes and buckets that crowded out every inch of floor space save for a winding, narrow little path from the counter to the door. On fine days the pressure for space spilled half of Trevor's wares outside onto the pavement, and under a canvas awning there would appear a teetering outdoor display of yard brushes, chimney brushes, hand brushes, shovels, spades, and garden rakes crammed into shiny galvanised dustbins.

I loved the intoxicating smell of Trevor's shop; a powerful aroma of glue and paint and turpentine, of paraffin and putty and linseed oil. People said that there was no type of ironmongery that Trevor did not stock, and that despite the welter of stuff heaped in confusion all around him, if you named what you needed he would, without hesitation, pick his way through the multitude of things and lay his hands right on the requested item, first time, every time.

Walk along Aberfan Road today and you will find just a couple of shops. Most of those that were there in the 1960s have been converted to houses or allowed to run to semi-dereliction. But back then everyone shopped in the village and there was a shop to meet every need.

I remember the post office and the postmaster; a man of solemn demeanour and scrupulous manners, he was bent almost to ninety degrees at his waist by some fearful deformity of the spine. The sight of him provoked in me an unbearable pity, a pity beyond the boundaries of what could be spoken as he stamped my mother's family allowance book with a tremendous 'thump-thump'. I developed a morbid fear that I would someday share the fate of his cruel disability, and whenever I thought of him I would try to stand up extra straight.

I recall the general grocer's shops; Collins', Harding's, the Co-op, and Pegler's: the poshest shop of all, with its high stools for tired customers to sit on, Cheddar cut with cheese wire on a marble slab, and cooked ham sliced electrically with a humming, shining circular blade after the discerning customer had specified the thickness of each slice. At Pegler's, each purchase was individually wrapped in greaseproof paper, the sales assistant neatly folding up the package in a blur of dexterity. Uniquely, the shop's name was enamelled onto big, white globular gas lamps which hung out over the street. No other shop had anything quite so swanky.

Rees' Chemist, however, came close with its Victorian mahogany counter and shelves and its ranks of shining apothecary jars full of mysterious substances and with (deliberately) indecipherable labels: POTASS:CARB:, CALC:CHLORID:, UNC:SULPH. If my mother had a prescription to cash, I'd wait impatiently amidst the smell of Germolene ointment and liniment rub, nagging my mother for a penny to put in the machine that you could weigh yourself on, or for a 'glucose' lolly, which, since they were sold in a chemist's shop, must surely have been good for me.

I can still feel the thrill of trying on my first pair of black slip-on daps for school in the shoe shop near Smyrna chapel and how I sniffed their heady smell of adhesive and brand new rubber in their brand new box, lined with tissue paper. The box was almost as exciting a prospect as the daps themselves, and before we had left the shop, I had already planned in my mind's eye the toy garage I would make from it to house my Dinky car collection.

Just opposite was Hughes' Newsagent ('Hughes the News', inevitably enough). This was run by my adult cousin, another Trevor, and his wife. Thrillingly this was the only shop in the village that sold two precious commodities: Airfix models and, between hard covers, abridged versions of children's classics. Just occasionally, I might manage to lay my hands on a 1:72 scale Spitfire or Messerschmitt Bf 109 which I'd painstakingly construct at our kitchen table with a tube of gloriously fragrant polystyrene cement and tiny tins of enamel paint smelling every bit as good as the glue. It was at Trevor's shop that I took possession of my first 'proper' book and I read and reread that abridged version of Jules Verne's *Twenty Thousand Leagues Under the Sea* until I had memorised long passages of it.

Down the road next to Berni's, there was a gas showroom which did good business as more and more people fitted gas cookers and fires to replace their coal ones. People queued amongst the shiny new appliances to pay the gas bill at the counter in the back. The great conversion from Town gas to North Sea gas was to happen soon.

Not far away, my Uncle Georgie, my grandmother's brother, had opened a tiny barber's shop (hence he was known to all as 'Georgie Barber' of course). Here, there were dozens of old boxing magazines scattered on the wooden kitchen-type chairs around the walls to read while you waited your turn and a framed photograph of Cassius Clay, cut from a magazine, in pride of place on the wall. Georgie's shop smelt strongly of Brylcreem and shaving soap, and was a quiet male refuge, the only sound generally being the click-clack of Georgie's scissors. There was a proper adjustable barber's chair with red leather upholstery, so big I had to sit boosted by a wooden box under my backside. Georgie was diminutive and mischievous. He had a salesman's patter and always ran through the options for haircuts with me with great seriousness as if I were the most discerning adult customer; the 'Short-Back-and-Sides', the 'Tony Curtis', the 'Slickback' and the 'Boston'.

'What'll it be then, lovely boy?' he'd ask.

'A Boston, please, Uncle Georgie.'

I always chose the Boston. I had not the remotest idea what a 'Boston' should look like, but I loved the sound of the word: American and modern. In reality it made no difference since I always ended up with, just like everyone else, a short-back-and-sides. I'm sure it was the only haircut that Georgie had actually mastered. It took me some while to figure this out.

A haircut at Georgie's was at least a short-lived affair, especially after he took delivery of some new electric clippers, and Georgie would have you in and out of that barber's chair in five minutes flat, flourishing a hand mirror to show the back of your shorn head. The doings at the women's hairdresser on Aberfan Road were a very different prospect. This was a place for small boys to avoid at all costs. On a few occasions Mam had no choice but to take me with her to get her hair done, and I soon learned that the maintenance of those beehives and bouffant styles of the 1960s and early 70s could become the work of an entire, interminable afternoon. I would sit there amid the enormous helmet-shaped hair dryers which whined incessantly, the sickly smells of lacquer and ammonia and peroxide all around, and with nothing to look at save the unreadable back copies of *Woman's Own* scattered about the salon. I sat and squirmed for what seemed like an eternity, the tedium driving me to the verge of tears, but afraid to shift from my seat for fear of showing up my mother.

'He's good as gold, Marion,' the women would say to her, and Mam would smile and nod as all the while I silently prayed for an escape, boiling and bubbling inside with boredom like a lidded saucepan.

There might eventually be a reward though. Perhaps a trip to the chip shop where I could order six pen'north of chips as a treat or a bag of 'bits' for a penny, and you could administer your own salt and vinegar and so always add too much. I loved the little wooden forks you could get for free.

In those days Aberfan Road also boasted a men's outfitter, a jeweller, a boutique (all women's clothes shops had suddenly become 'boutiques'), two bank branches, a haberdasher and the other branch of Stone's Family Butcher. Squeezed in between somehow were two pubs: the Aberfan Hotel and the Mackintosh Hotel which were not either of them really hotels at all, as well as, at the very northern end of the street, the Aberfan Social Democratic Club, named for the old Marxist Social Democratic Federation, one of the founding associates of the Labour Party at its foundation, back in 1900.

Any adult, and not just one's parents, was quite likely to call to you as you played in the street to ask for an errand to be run, with a reward on offer of thruppence, or even a tanner, should you accept the job. It never occurred to me to refuse. In just the same way it was usual, if one was thirsty, for instance, to ask at any door for a drink of water and in all likelihood to be offered a 'piece' (of bread and butter) to go with it. All adults known by name held the honorific prefix of 'Aunty' or 'Uncle', and we children moved in and out of each other's houses freely, admiring and envying each other's toys and being fed jam or mashed banana sandwiches and drinks of squash in plastic beakers by one another's parents. It was as if, as children, although we had our own family of course, we were also to some extent held in common. Each of us everyone's concern. Years later while at secondary school, I recall overhearing a conversation between two teachers. One was warning the other to be wary of kids from Aberfan because they'd all been 'spoiled' and that this was one of the consequences of the disaster. That wasn't true. That wasn't it at all. All Valleys communities were close and I'm sure almost anyone of my generation would testify to that. I think it was just that, for the adults of Aberfan back then, that closeness was a little more knowing. A little more necessary.

When I was around eight years old, a real aunt of mine, my great Aunty Kitty, Lily's sister, moved into Wingfield Street, one of the 'side streets' off Cottrell Street. She'd been temporarily rehoused after the disaster in a council house in Pantglas Fawr at the far northern end of Aberfan, because her original home in Moy Road had been completely destroyed. Kitty had no children and now lived alone since her husband, Dick, had been killed on that October day in 1966.

Kitty was tiny. Around four foot ten. She was also feisty, with short curly hair dyed red. I thought she looked a little like a picture of Queen Elizabeth I that I had once seen in a Ladybird book, minus the ruff around her neck of course, and the bejewelled frock.

Kitty claimed – her fists raised – that she could box, though I never took her up on her frequent offers to spar with me as I was half convinced she was telling the truth. She could also dance the Charleston and showed us how, now and then, in her new kitchen, her stockinged feet jinking on the oilcloth-covered floor. I ran a lot of errands for Kitty. Over time I got the idea that she was so often to be found standing on her doorstep deliberately because she was hoping to catch me as I passed so she could ask me to grab some milk or bread from the shops. I began slowly to realise that she was herself sometimes reluctant to leave the house. She would look up anxiously at the sky if she so much as took a step outside her front door. As the years passed, this problem became more and more pronounced. Looking back, I'm sure that agoraphobia was consolidating its grip on her.

One heavy summer afternoon at her house, having just returned from the shops at her request, I was sitting at her kitchen table drinking a glass of milk and dunking custard cream biscuits while she chatted cheerfully away. She was always giving me the news on our complicated network of cousins. Without warning, there was a clap of thunder. A big, booming rumble that had windows trembling in their sashes as it echoed up the valley. I was startled, as anyone would be, and craned my neck to look out of her back window to check for rain or lightning I suppose. There is always something thrilling about a summer storm. By the time I had refocused my attention on the room, just a second or two later, Kitty was gone. I did a double take, bewildered. Then I heard her rapid breathing and looking down saw that she was huddled on all fours, shaking mightily, hidden beneath the kitchen table. Her eyes were rolling. Having never seen an adult behave like this,

I took her actions to be some kind of practical joke she was playing on me. That would not have been so out of character for Kitty. So I burst out laughing. A genuine belly laugh. Kitty did not move. She did not laugh in return. My stomach turned over as I realised she was genuinely terrified, shaking with fear at the sound of thunder. I had never seen an adult afraid like that before. It was some while before I managed to coax her out again from under that table; at eight years old I was new to reassuring adults who showed fear.

Later, I told my Dad what had happened and he simply said that some people were afraid of thunder and that for Kitty's sake I shouldn't talk about it. I didn't, and that was that.

Many years later, however, when I was in my thirties, over a drink in the Social Club, my father, unprompted, began to talk about his experiences on the day of the disaster. This was to be the only time he spoke of it to me. Among other things, he related what he knew about Kitty's story.

She and her husband, Dick Jones, were at home that morning in their house in Moy Road, just across the road from Pantglas Junior School. Kitty was upstairs, and Dick was in the living room lighting the fire when the house was hit by the deluge of slurry. The house collapsed on top of them. Dick was killed. Kitty was trapped, alive, in some air pocket created by the randomness of the destruction. When rescuers began to arrive they hurled themselves and their effort, understandably so, at the wreckage of the school in the hope that some of the children could be saved as indeed, at least very early on, some were. The school and the children came first in everyone's mind. No one really attempted digging into the wreckage of the houses nearby for quite some time and so Kitty lay undiscovered all that while. During that time the fire Dick had been lighting had started to spread, smouldering amidst the wreckage and, close by her, Dick's body was caught in that fire. Kitty was conscious all this time and knew exactly what was happening. It was some hours before rescuers heard her calls for help.

Whilst Kitty was lying trapped under the rubble of her home, my father was less than a hundred yards away amongst the volunteer rescuers clawing at the wreckage of Pantglas School. At first there were only picks and shovels to dig with. Miners from Merthyr Vale Colliery soon began to arrive and used their expertise to bring better coordination to the efforts to shift rubble, wreckage, and the still moving mass of slurry which was by then some ten metres deep in the immediate area of the school. More miners from Deep Navigation and Taff Merthyr collieries a few miles down the valley arrived soon after. Police from Merthyr joined the early rescue efforts. Periodically, my father related, someone would call for silence and for a while the digging stopped so that everyone might listen in the hush for sounds of life beneath the debris and the muck. The tip had begun its slide down the mountain at around 9.15 that morning, just as the teachers in the school had begun taking the register. Despite the desperate efforts of what eventually became a total of around two thousand rescue workers, no one was pulled out alive after 11am.

It gradually became clear that the grim and heart breaking work of all concerned was turning into an effort to recover bodies.

My father was asked by the police to join a group of men who would receive the bodies as they were uncovered. It was this experience, as he told me all those years later, that was the hardest to bear. Out of sight of the crowds of parents and other relatives that had gathered round, in a part of the school that was relatively intact, this small group took the little bodies that were brought to them, still coated in filth and slurry, and wrapped them carefully in blankets.

By 2.30pm, the police Regional Crime Squad had set up a temporary mortuary in Bethania Chapel just a few hundred yards away. The children's bodies, still wrapped in their blankets, were laid on stretchers and passed hand over hand to begin their journey to Bethania. Here, amidst the all-pervading smell of disinfectant, in the Sunday School room at the rear of the chapel, the bodies were washed clean and labelled with a number at wrist and ankle and then wrapped once more in clean blankets. Their clothing and property were placed in plastic bags.

The children's bodies were small enough to be laid directly onto the chapel pews. This was where their parents would find them, when they were admitted two groups at a time, and were asked to identify their child or children.

This process began that same afternoon. Many parents waited patiently in line to be admitted, only to be unable to identify their child. This meant that the body was yet to be recovered from the school. These parents rejoined the line outside the chapel to wait again, in the rain. Some went through this process repeatedly, fathers and mothers taking turns, standing in line through day and night, waiting for another attempt to find their child. The last body was identified fifteen days later.

Thirty years had passed before my father told me about at least some of what he had witnessed on the day of the disaster and during the days that followed. Even then I was aware that he held a great deal back. After all, some of the bodies were identified only when the police lifted fingerprints from favourite children's toys in order to corroborate dental records.

'No one should have to see what we saw,' he told me.

My generation, a few years younger than the victims, was never sat down and simply told about what had happened to our community, or to our families. At least that has been my experience. Facts emerged for us gradually, in snippets of related memory, like shards of glass from a broken window. Just as the window cannot be pieced back together, the complete picture, the lived experience of so many, cannot ever be fully known. The survivors, the bereaved and the witnesses, all hold a part of the picture in their memory, but each holds the tragedy entire and whole in their hearts.

Just four years ago, in 2012, another jagged piece of the story of Aberfan presented itself to me unbidden whilst I was visiting the Big Pit National Coal Museum in Blaenavon with my own children. We had visited the museum several times already by then, and it remains for us a favourite family destination for a day out. I took a look at the part of the permanent exhibition that tells the story of Aberfan, as I had done on every other occasion I had been there. But this time I looked right into the eyes of my father. He was right there before me, in a photograph reproduced from the front page of the *Western Mail* and dated the day after the disaster. There he was, standing atop a heap of slurry and the wreckage of Pantglas School. In the photograph he is still wearing his jacket and tie from work and he is leaning on the garden spade that my mother had thrown to him that morning. He seems to be catching his breath, and he is looking directly at the camera. It is difficult to read the expression on his face, his features washed out by the poor newsprint reproduction of photographs in those days, but there is no doubt that it is him. He looks so improbably young.

It is a curious thing, for I had looked at that photograph several times already on previous visits, without ever noticing him specifically amongst the dozens of other men scrambling and digging in the ruins. And so another part of his experience and my earliest memory suddenly slotted into place, so many years later.

And so it was, too, when near to forty years on, my Uncle Wyndham supplied to me, in passing, the piece of information which explained Kitty's fear that day in her kitchen, on the day of the summer storm. He told me that in the instant before the house collapsed around herself and her husband, Kitty had mistaken the roar of the landslide for the sound of thunder.

# A Year's Turning

As I grew and my understanding slowly broadened, I saw that as well as the weekly rhythm of home and school, of Saturday cinema and Sunday chapel, there was the great slow rhythm of the whole long year, punctuated by festivals and holidays that marked the passage of my childhood days.

The arrival of spring was signalled by St David's Day, a half-day holiday at school and in those days, at least in our part of Wales, a festival with which only schools were much bothered. There were songs to be learned in Welsh, weeks in advance, the words memorised through repetition without any grasp, or explanation, of their meaning. There was '*Hen Wlad Fy Nhadau*' of course, '*Oes gafr eto?*' with its accelerating beat, and my favourite: '*Suo Gan*', a lullaby which then, as now, can bring a genuine tear to my eye, especially when sung by children. We dressed up for all this; the girls in their tall black hats and red plaid skirts and shawls and we boys, there being no real defined national costume for our sex, hazily Welshified by addition of our granddads' 'Dai caps', a scarf and waistcoat and little green and white felt leeks on our lapels that we had made for ourselves in class, held together with glue and a safety pin. One particularly fine 1st March, I remember the whole affair was conducted outdoors beneath the flagpole in front of the school, the Red Dragon flying aloft. When we had finished our singing we were each presented with a medal in a plastic pocket with the Prince of Wales' three feathers in silver superimposed on red enamel. It was for the 'Investiture' said Mrs Jones, our headmistress. I had no idea what that was, but I loved the deep red colour of the enamel, and decided that from then on, that would be my favourite colour if anyone were ever to ask. We lined up behind a bed of daffodils and we had our picture taken.

Around this time of year there came, also, the most dreaded of all annual events: the chapel anniversary. This special service involved the Sunday School 'scholars' learning what we termed a 'piece', for performance in front of assembled parents, grandparents, aunties and uncles. Although for the older children this might involve a hymn sung as a solo or something performed on a musical instrument, for us younger ones this generally meant a recitation of a 'verse', a short poem, in front of a packed congregation of mothers and fathers and grandparents. This was terrifying enough but the rub was this: the verse had to be memorised and not read out. Weeks prior to Anniversary Sunday we were handed our verse handwritten on a sheet of lined paper by one of our Sunday School teachers in a neat, cursive style. Almost immediately, we scrambled to compare them with one another, desperate to seek out and swap our own for better-prized examples that might be shorter than the others, by a line, or even a single word, since the shorter the piece, the easier it would be to memorise, and the quicker it would be to perform. We needn't have fussed. No amount of cajolery, confectionery-based bribery, or even tearful pleading would ever separate the lucky winner of a shorter piece from their prize. And so followed the long process of learning by rote. I would do this with eyes clamped shut, the piece of paper soon much crumpled and eventually semi-transparent through long hours clasped in sweaty palms, held behind my back.

When the day came we each waited, dressed in our best, for our turn in the proceedings. We gathered round the *sedd mawr* like little aristocrats at the foot of the guillotine, all filled with fearful nerves and trying not to show it. Then, of a sudden, it was up to the pulpit, a breathless gabble through the words, eyes fixed on the back wall of the chapel, and then a hurried, undignified, scuttling return to the anonymity of the pews, settling down with a heartfelt sigh of relief as attention shifted to the next victim. Never once during those performances did I have the gumption to look my mother or father in the eye during a recitation, such was the extent of my mortification. But here it was, done, and thank heavens for it. For another year, at least.

Each year, as near to Mayday as made no difference, a travelling fair came to the village. All of it packed and ingeniously folded on the back of lorries belching diesel fumes in convoy, with electric generators on wheels and caravans for the workforce and owners. Overnight, while we slept, the rides and stalls were unfurled like reverse origami and by the morning when we woke, there they were, installed on the waste ground behind the old library, hatched out like multi-coloured mayflies in the spring morning.

There were wooden swing boats to be worked by the riders themselves, hauling on ropes, a shooting gallery with air rifles and slug pellets, and stalls to hook-a-duck or spear a playing card with three darts with goldfish for prizes. There was a waltzer too, but by far the best and biggest attraction were the dodgems. Truth be told, all seemed a little forlorn in broad daylight with faded paint and metal struts all chipped and scratched. But as evening fell and darkness settled around the stalls and rides, cloaking all imperfections, everything was transformed. All became intriguing, as the generators burped and rumbled into life and the hundreds of multi-coloured low-wattage light bulbs festooned about the site gently fizzed into life. Then the music started up, and buzzing loudspeakers began to belt out numbers by Slade and T Rex and the Bay City Rollers at full volume, rattling windows in the houses round about and setting the elderly to openly tutting and quietly blaspheming. And soon, moth-like, all the children and teenagers of Aberfan and Merthyr Vale and from the other villages round about emerged from the spring dark, drawn irresistibly to this new particoloured puddle of light. They circled round the stalls and rides again and again, tramping across the rutted muddy site in search of entertainment and, in the case of the teenagers, of each other.

As I joined them, I was fascinated by this lighting up of the night, and looked up to the sky now made an even deeper black than was usual, and holding a deeper silence than on any ordinary night, through its contrast with the bubble of light and sound that enclosed us. The smell of fried onions from the hot dog stand wafted through the press of bodies, and set my mouth to watering as it mingled with the odour of burnt sugar expelled by the candy floss machine that whirred pink cobweb strands around long sticks. Girls on the waltzer screamed for effect and the dodgems sparked and rumbled.

We never had enough money to try more than a ride or two, but once I won a goldfish in a water-filled plastic bag and Allyson managed to claim a coconut somehow. I demolished a hot dog awash with greasy onions and watched as the older boys crashed the dodgem cars together with as much violence as they could muster by way of impressing girls.

As I was still young, I was rounded up after an hour or so to head back home, and gradually the fair was left to the teenagers and their flirting. On the way home I tackled some candy floss which melted into little ruby droplets in my mouth and on my lips as I buried my face in the pink, wispy, sticky fluff.

Back at home, while the bass notes of the music and the soprano screech of girls on the waltzer still sounded out, loud enough to penetrate our closed windows, Mam installed my goldfish in an old, water-filled sweetie jar. Dad tackled the coconut with a hammer and a six-inch nail, knocking in holes so each of us could sample the thin milk inside. It tasted soapy, and disappointing somehow – I don't know what I was expecting. Dad then broke the shell by whacking it on the back doorstep and we scraped the flesh from the inside surface with our teeth.

On waking next morning, I found my goldfish floating belly up in the sweetie jar, stone dead. Allyson said she wasn't surprised because she knew for certain Gareth had come downstairs in the middle of the night and peed in the water. He denied this vigorously. Whatever the truth of it, I was a little relieved, since I couldn't see the point of goldfish, and wasn't relishing the thought of looking after one. Now, if it had been a puppy, that would have been different.

Within three days the fairground was packed and gone. And that particular and unique crowd of children that it had made was scattered, never to be reassembled.

In the years immediately following the disaster, Aberfan and Merthyr Vale became even closer communities than they had been before, if that were possible. They also became even more active and even better organised. A plethora of committees, church groups, youth clubs, sports clubs and social groups were set up, all interconnected and involving most local people in some way or another. The Young Wives group was formed, with many of the bereaved mothers, grandmothers and their friends becoming involved. The Young Wives became a haven. A place of companionship and of unique understanding, a place where grief was acknowledged in all its corrosive potency, but also a place where life, even alongside grief, was allowed to make headway. The group endures to this day.

All these groups were formed from a spontaneous, communal urge amongst people to come together and to find and offer support amidst the grieving. Grieving that would be lifelong.

One amongst these groups was the Carnival Committee, set up to organise a summer carnival each year, and on a grand scale. At the heart of the event was a grand parade of floats where each street would compete with their neighbour streets for first prize. Our team was 'Cottrell Street and side streets'. Devotees of the float competition could be competitive in the extreme. Once a theme was chosen, top secret preparations could begin long before the carnival itself, with prefabricated sections being made for final transfer to the flat-bed lorry that carried the scenery and participants in the parade. All out of sight of potential spies from other streets, people wrestled with acres of cardboard, hundreds of rolls of Bacofoil, gallons of paint and thousands of individually made tissue paper flowers in many colours, which for some reason were considered indispensable to any decent float. Costumes for those riding the float (almost all of them children) would be run up, and the more elaborate they were, the better. Any theme could be chosen. The Wild West, Outer Space, and a South Sea Island all made appearances. The year I remember best our theme was 'The Homepride Flour Men'. I was one of the kids decked out in little black suits and bowler hats, just like the little cartoon men in the TV adverts. It was a fiercely hot day that year, and the full-sized, real bowler that I was wearing, padded out with newspaper to make it fit, steadily roasted my head as we made our slow procession through the streets, cheered on by people with their kitchen chairs brought out onto the pavements to watch. 'Graded Grains Make Finer Flour' it said on the top of the float, spelled out in the ubiquitous tissue-paper flowers. The floats would be accompanied by children and adults in fancy dress (another prize at stake) entered singly or in groups. The outstanding all time winning entry was Mary 'milk-the-bull', a lady of, let us say, goodly proportions who squeezed herself somehow into a Wonder Woman costume, complete with whip, with which she lashed any would-be Lothario who got too close. Or any that tried to run away, come to that. There would be at least six 'jazz bands' along for the ride. These bands, having little enough to do with actual jazz music, were made up of troupes of teenage girls in matching homemade uniforms who belted out tunes, both popular and classical, at deafening volume on enormous kazoos to the accompaniment of drummers bringing up the rear. There was a prize for the best jazz band too. We wound our way like this, slowly, round as many streets of the two villages as possible to the carnival field where the refreshment stalls, amusements, the Mayor and the judges all awaited us.

Each year a celebrity would be invited to do the honours of officially opening the carnival with a speech made over an unreliable public address system. On one occasion the celebrity was Douglas Bader, the World War Two flying ace famously portrayed by Kenneth More in the movie *Reach for the Sky*. This was a great thrill for us boys for it was still a time when boys devoured stories of wartime derring-do in the comics that we hoarded and swapped. Here was a real live hero. For weeks after the event we tried to copy Bader's characteristic gait as he walked on his prosthetic legs across our carnival field. There was no mockery in it. We thought it genuinely cool.

After the speeches, we gorged on sandwiches and Welsh cakes and orange squash. Big men with sledgehammers smashed outworn pianos in competition against the clock, creating tremendous jangling noises which echoed and re-echoed off the mountainsides on each side of the valley. There was a ferocious tug-of-war tournament, the competitors straining and wheezing whilst ploughing furrows with their heels. Then, more cups and medals were presented to the various jazz bands. All of us children ran about and caught the sun, so that next day we would be peeling the skin from our noses, and Wonder Woman, naturally, won first prize in the fancy dress.

The year of the Homepride Flour Graders, we won second prize in the float competition. In fact, 'Cottrell Street and side streets' seemed to come second every year. And Moy Road always seemed to come first. Someone behind me muttered, 'Bloody Moy Road again.'

Despite the attractions of the carnival, no summertime event was half so eagerly anticipated as the annual chapel trip to Barry Island. We signed up weeks in advance on Sunday

School mornings, each of us handing over an envelope with a few two shilling pieces inside, scrunched tightly in our hands for fear of loss. This was our contribution to the day, our mothers having set it aside in stages (almost as soon as having saved up enough for this, our mothers would again begin the whole process of 'putting something by' in preparation for Christmas).

When the great day finally arrived, we gathered just after dawn on a Saturday outside the chapel at the bottom of Bridge Street, the early start being deemed necessary in order to get the best out of the day. It also took a lot longer to get to Barry and back in those days than it does today. Mam, having a morbid fear of lateness and of any form of ill-preparedness, had been up since the early hours of the morning, cutting sandwiches filled with tinned salmon, or cheese, or jam, and wrapping them, separately according to filling, into little cooking foil parcels. These, together with a couple of empty pop bottles refilled with orange squash, some plastic beakers, a Thermos flask of sugared tea, our swimming costumes, towels, and that pungent-smelling sun tan oil that no one uses any more, were crammed into string bags. Here was everything we needed to see us through the day.

In the early light, the air cool at this time of day, the village was quiet save for some half-hearted birdsong, until growling over the bridge came two elderly coaches, labouring hard, and eventually juddering to a halt beside us, their diesel engines throbbing: our charabancs had arrived. Cyril Vaughan, one of the Sunday School teachers, moved amongst the press of bodies ticking names off a list. There were at least a hundred of us; children and mothers, grannies, aunties, great aunties, and honorific aunties too (the adult males having decided that this day was a perfect opportunity to stay at home and relish some peace and quiet). Boys pushed to the fore, and a ragged cheer went up as the doors of the coaches pivoted open.

'Morning, Drive!' each of us called out in turn as we stampeded aboard (not to greet the driver in this idiom would have been considered very bad form).

'Not too far back, now!' Mam called out to Gareth and me, but the back seat had already been 'bagsied' by the older boys plus Allyson who, now a teenager, considered her younger brothers a mortifying embarrassment. Gareth and I jumped on two neighbouring seats to save one for Mam and for Anne, who never knew what elbows were for, and would inevitably be last inside.

'Remember which coach we're on, now,' said Mam, already anxious about the return journey before we had even set off. Since there were only two coaches in any case, it wasn't going to be too difficult to sort out. The coaches turned about-face at the end of Cottrell Street and we were off, bouncing over the bridge, roaring past the pit head baths and canteen, and speeding past the 'Daggers' ex-servicemen's club, where Dada drank, even though he wasn't an ex-serviceman at all. We made it all the way over the level crossing and almost to the top of Bell's Hill before the first of the children was sick. A small plastic bucket that had been brought along by one of the mothers, wisely prepared for this inevitability, was whipped from hand to hand in time to catch the worst of it.

We chuntered on southwards along Cardiff Road, the sun still low enough to make us squint, but strong enough already to begin warming the upholstery of the seats which gave off an aroma of old cigarette smoke and faux leather, all mixed up with a whiff of diesel fumes. Excited chatter filled the bus, boys wriggling and bouncing on their seats, the women gossiping and teasing the driver as well as each other. Leaving the valley was a rarity for me then, and once we passed through Quakers Yard and struck out towards Cilfynydd and Pontypridd we were, as far as many of us were concerned, on foreign territory, and the talk and chatter grew a little more subdued as we left behind the familiar geography of hills and terraced streets. Soon we skirted round Cardiff and entered the Vale of Glamorgan and had sight of clean green fields, scattered houses with front gardens and here and there a thatched cottage, like a picture on a jigsaw box.

We drove by Llandough hospital on its hill, and before long we were on our way through Barry itself. We drove along streets of Victorian town houses that seemed to me unfeasibly vast, like two normal houses stacked one atop the other, and passed bungalows with cars parked on driveways, and neat, neat gardens with lawns just for show. Then our little convoy made its way across the causeway, the railway line running alongside us, and onto Barry Island proper.

We came to a halt in the car park near the railway sidings that smelled of dust and diesel, and we spilled out of the coach in a muddle of mothers, aunties, baggage, and rolled up towels. There was a brief confusion as families regrouped, and then we struck out for the seafront in a gabbling procession. The sun here shone brighter than at home, horizons being wider now we had left our hillsides behind. The smell of the sea grew stronger, fusing with the sharp odours of vinegar and frying chips and the fishy stink of cockles, whelks and winkles being sold from stalls along the seafront.

At last we stood on the sand-strewn promenade and took in the scene. There were striped canvas deckchairs for hire, hundreds of them, stacked like plates on a draining board, alongside penny-in-the-slot telescopes for looking over to England, and a great big public toilet that smelled faintly of pee and strongly of disinfectant – a state of affairs which would reverse itself as the day wore on. Behind us were the amusement arcades, open to the street and already pumping out loud music that competed in volume with the dings and thuds of pinball machines and one-armed-bandits, and before us was the beach, its arc of sand already heaving with thousands of bodies. The tide was out, and a wide flat world awaited us, all the way down to the churning brown waters of the Bristol Channel.

The mothers and aunties each hired a deckchair and hauled them down onto the sandy beach to seek out a prime spot as near as possible to the esplanade wall, so as to be near the gift shops and ice cream stands. When they had found a free patch of sand a few yards square they installed the deckchairs in a circle, facing inward, like a wagon train settling for the night. This was our staked claim of sand, a little patch of Aberfan away from home, and our communal headquarters for the day. Immediately, Thermos flasks of hot sweet tea were produced from the bulging bags of towels and sandwiches, and the mothers and aunties set to gossiping and laughing whilst sipping the tea from plastic cups.

Mam installed a couple of deckchairs for us, and Anne flopped into one and began to read a book while Gareth and I wriggled out of our shorts and sandals and into our swimming costumes whilst dancing with a towel wrapped around our waists for the sake of modesty. Allyson was already bored with childish company and mooched off in search of the other big kids from the back seat of the bus. Before we were let loose,

Mam insisted on applying sun tan oil onto our shoulders and backs. I don't know what that stuff was, but it smelled evil and vinegary and was doled out from an unmarked medicine bottle. It must have been homemade, and was certainly of dubious worth.

At long last we were released, and my brother ran with me full tilt across the sand. At first all was fluffy and dry and hot underfoot, with embedded sprigs of dried out bladderwrack pricking our toes, then the ground grew wetter and cooler and flatter as we steadily closed the distance between us and the sea. Behind us the promenade dwindled, already far away, and the grown-ups dwindled with it, and the world became an upturned bowl of blue. Our feet pattered fast on the wet sand, gulls screeched, the breeze picked up and we hurled ourselves into a world without obstacle or boundary. We hit the sea at full speed, splashing in awkwardly, lifting our knees high to overstep the first wavelets. The cold of the water was stunning. It didn't seem possible that on a day so warm, this water could be so cold. So we kicked the freezing spray in each other's faces, howling and laughing, and the salty taste crept in at the corner of my mouth and stung my eyes. Then it was time to try our courage and wade out deeper, and I gasped as the cold, cold water reached my waist. I flopped down onto my backside and let the water close over my head, just for a second, but long enough to open my eyes underwater, as I'd promised myself I would, just to see what it was like. I glimpsed nothing but a muddy brown fog, and shot back to my feet, spitting and spluttering, snot running from my nose. When the cold water became too much to bear we combed the shore for treasure but found little; this ground had been well searched by hundreds of other kids already. There were bits of seaweed lying about like scraps of rotting black lace, and here and there were empty limpet shells and bottle tops studding the wet sand. Gareth turned up a collection of disarticulated crabs' legs poking skywards from the sand like fingers beckoning.

Later, back at the deckchairs, we nagged Mam to buy us a bucket and spade – the proper metal spades and not the plastic ones meant for babies. Eventually she relented and bought us one set between us. Almost immediately, Gareth cut his foot on the metal's edge, and began to bleed impressively into the sand. My mother being my mother, he was soon sorted out with antiseptic and a sticking plaster, and I got the bucket and spade to myself for a while, until my brother gathered enough courage to try again.

At lunchtime we opened our cooking foil parcels and munched tinned salmon sandwiches gritty with sand, and drank lukewarm squash from our plastic beakers – there was sand in that too.

There was a funfair on Barry Island, but money was short and so the grown-ups always planned things (I discovered years later) so that we visited it only when there was just an hour left before the buses would leave to take us home. I had other ideas and headed to the amusement arcade with my designated allocation of pennies. Here they had the one-armed-bandits that my grandmother had warned me against but that I thought boring anyway. There were old arcade games that fired little ball bearings round a metal track to score points, and a penny-in-the-slot haunted house that played the same scene over and over with little automata; a man sat by his fire reading a newspaper while a ghost crept up on him, and when he saw it his hair flew up like a levitating wig. There was a 'what the butler saw' machine that I was too nervous to try in case anyone saw me, and grabbing claw machines stuffed with fluffy toys that you could never hope to win, but my favourite was a submarine warfare game which involved squinting into a periscope and launching torpedoes across a night-time ocean to sink ships silhouetted on the horizon. If you got it just right, the ships gave out a satisfying flash and boom and sank beneath the waves.

Later, we all met back at a café opposite the car park for the final treat of the day: a knickerbocker glory served in a tall glass with a cherry on top and a chewing gum ball lurking at the bottom, buried in ice cream and raspberry syrup. At first they seemed too big to eat, but we battled our way through them with our long handled spoons, and claimed our chewing gum prizes.

We gathered back at the coaches with sand grating the flesh between our toes and Cyril Vaughan opened the boot of the bus and broke into our supplies for the homeward journey. Each child was handed a packet of salt and vinegar crisps and a bottle of 'Zing', a fizzy drink, livid red in colour and with a taste as sharp as battery acid. We clambered aboard and set off, and had barely made it to the other end of the Barry Island causeway before the ice cream, crisps and fizzy pop had done their work and the cry went up for the little plastic bucket once again.

We settled in for the long journey home, woozy in the stuffy heat of the bus and bone tired after a day of sea air. The little ones and the grannies snoozed as the coach growled its way back through Barry, and through the Vale, and when at long last we passed the winding gear of Abercynon Colliery, I knew we were back home in the Valleys again. The coaches dropped us where we had begun, outside the chapel; each child in turn piping up, 'Thank you, drive!' as we disembarked. The street lamps were winking into life as we gathered our belongings, tired goodbyes were said, and we all walked home with weary legs, our shoulders itchy beneath our shirts.

I slept that night the deep, deep sleep that only children truly know, and that likely only children truly deserve.

Next morning, we children woke with agonising sunburn across our backs and shoulders. Mam sat us on the kitchen table and dabbed our flame-red skin with calamine lotion as we whimpered and twitched in pain. For the next few days, morbidly fascinated, we peeled the skin off each other's shoulders in long strips as it sloughed itself away.

Summer turned to autumn and at weekends we often set out, armed with old biscuit tins, to go blackberrying. This free harvest could be found all around the village, at the side of paths up to the mountain and along the canal 'bank', which marked the route of the old Merthyr/Cardiff canal, long since filled in. We picked for hours, searching for the biggest and juiciest specimens, which of course never made it to the tin and were eaten immediately after checking them for grubs. All of us collected dozens of nettle stings too, and we rubbed our bare legs with dock leaves to ease the itchy pain. The berries that did make it back home were baked into tarts by my grandmother, with steaming, slightly soggy pastry, and we ate them coated with sugar and doused with evaporated milk, or with sterilised cream from a tin.

School started up again and the mornings grew colder, that thrilling, expectant autumn chill in the air. Nana knitted me another cable-stitch jumper, one with the same green wool from the wool shop on Aberfan Road. I was fond of this one too, and wondered whether green might not be my favourite colour after all. All the boys at school developed a craze for playing conkers. These were precious, since there was not a single horse chestnut tree in Aberfan, and supplies had to be imported from the neighbouring village of Troedyrhiw. I swapped comics for a supply of half a dozen, and I spent a good deal of time admiring their silky, mahogany patina, rolling them satisfyingly between finger and thumb and polishing them on my sleeve. My grandfather showed me how to toughen them in the oven of the kitchen stove. After that I became unbeatable, at least for a while. When I eventually saw my champion 'forty-er' shatter and succumb, I was devastated. So I tried too my grandfather's alternative method of soaking them in vinegar in a jam jar, but I left them there too long and they turned soft and mushy and began to stink, floating in their fouled vinegar like anatomical specimens.

Halloween then was not the consumerist event it is today, and sometimes went unmarked altogether, but I remember that on at least one occasion, Mam laboured long and hard to make Halloween lanterns out of swedes. No one I knew had ever seen a pumpkin; they appeared only as images on imported American TV shows, and seemed impossibly large and fanciful things. I half suspected they were not real at all, or that what we saw on TV were cartoon-like exaggerations of whatever a real pumpkin might look like. We put burning candle stumps in our lanterns and turned off the living room light to watch them flicker in the dark. Soon the rancid smell of scorched swede filled the house. We ducked for apples in a plastic bowl placed on the middle room floor in front of the fire. Allyson won every time. She was fearless about plunging her face in the water. Gareth was almost as good as her, despite the absence of his front teeth.

In the run up to bonfire night we made a guy from an old pair of Dad's trousers and a threadbare shirt, with an old pillowcase for a head, all stuffed with balls of crumpled newspaper. It wore a grinning moustachioed mask we bought in Terry Martin's shop. Huge bonfires were constructed on any old piece of waste ground, youngsters organised by groupings of streets coming together in an unofficial contest to build the biggest. Teenage lads regularly raided the efforts of the competition after dark, bearing off their booty of fuel to be added to their own pyre. Old tyres were most prized as fuel as they burned for ages, the wires inside them twanging free as the flames ate away the rubber, sending up billowing clouds of sulphurous black smoke. Steadily, the bonfires grew with the addition of old furniture, mattresses, carpets and oilcloth flooring, once, even, an old piano. When 5th November finally arrived, each bonfire was festooned with not one but several guys, then doused in paraffin and set alight. We danced about the flames, the monstrous heat in our faces, and watched sparks spiral upwards into the November night. Bonfire night always seemed to be an occasion when there was more licence for kids to run a little wild, and we dashed frantically to and fro, trying even at this late stage to scavenge anything burnable within reach and hurl it into the flames, anything to augment and prolong the burning.

Older boys lurked on the edge of the bonfire's halo of light, half in and half out of the dark, and set off bangers and jumping jacks, just like the ones our teachers had warned us against. We little ones begged for sparklers and swirled them in the air and grew tearful when the supply ran out. Dad had a Catherine Wheel that he nailed to a fence post. He did this, as he did everything, with enormous care and, so it seemed to us children, at an agonisingly slow pace. He gave it several practise spins with his finger, and only when completely satisfied, did he light the fuse. When the fuse burned down, the Catherine Wheel obstinately refused to spin at all. It fizzed angrily but remained entirely stationary on its post until, at last, it broke completely loose, bounced on the ground and hurtled off at ankle height, away from the crowd, mercifully enough, and in the direction of the river. It hit the water at high speed, where it steamed and bubbled for an age until it finally succumbed and was swallowed by the wet and the dark. We stood on the riverbank and cheered. That could not possibly have gone any better, I thought, far better than just spinning on a post.

The supply of fireworks was soon exhausted and so we turned our attention back to the bonfire and we grew calmer as we all stared into the flames, watching as the fire collapsed in slow stages, each time sending another flurry of sparks upward into the night. The grown-ups passed round plastic cups of soup poured from Thermos flasks, and we scoured the ground for burned-out firework casings that we prodded with sticks. Later, when the fire had burned down a little more, we tried to roast potatoes wrapped in foil amongst the embers. It never worked. They were always scorched on the outside and raw in the middle.

We had built our bonfire on the derelict land next to Dickie Rees' breeze block factory, and we could see across the valley to the tram road in Merthyr Vale where their bigger, better bonfire was burning away. We could see up to Bryn Taff too, where the flames from their truly enormous edifice shot into the sky higher than the three-storey backs of the houses. Their bonfire was, after all, bigger than a house to begin with. Bryn Taff always managed to pinch more fuel than anyone else.

That night I went to sleep still able to smell the metallic smoke of the sparklers which I had waved against the dark, and with the aftertaste of tinned vegetable soup still in my mouth. I dreamed of our entire valley top to bottom, dotted with bonfires defying the night.

The days grew shorter yet and in the run-up to Christmas we made, at school, cardboard cutout, life-sized figures of the characters in the Nativity story. I helped make the donkey that carried Mary to Bethlehem. I spent an age cutting out pieces of grey plastic sponge, to represent the donkey's coat, which I then glued to a piece of donkey-shaped, donkey-sized cardboard. The figures were hung around the walls of the main hall in time for our carol concert.

In our chapel Nativity play, I was chosen to be one of the three kings and I wore a robe made from an old curtain and a cardboard crown, and I carried solemnly before me a painted cardboard box with sticky paper jewels studded all over it. It was empty, but there was meant to be frankincense inside it, and I wondered what on earth frankincense was.

Our father worked at the Hoover factory while our Uncle Wyndham was a surface worker at the pit. This allowed Anne, Allyson, Gareth and I to attend the two big 'works' Christmas parties that were held in the run up to the big day.

The annual miners' children's Christmas party was held in the miners' club in Merthyr Vale. Standing right opposite my maternal grandparents' house, the club was a Brutalist building that had its main entrance level with the street at Bryn Teg, but because the land beneath and behind it sloped away so steeply, most of the building was suspended in mid air, held up on spindly concrete pillars invisible from the roadway. Even as a relatively new building, it seemed to perch without any certain intent on that hillside, like all of Bryn Teg.

Hundreds of us would turn up for the party, and we were sat together in the main hall at trestle tables covered with paper tablecloths, our chairs jammed together so tightly there was barely room to move. The food was always good. A slice of ham and a bag of proper chip shop chips from the Windsor fish and chip shop just down the road, washed down with orange squash that tasted of the plastic bottle it came in. There was jelly for dessert, and we ate amidst the hoppy whiff of beer seeping in from the lounge bar next door. We were encouraged to entreat Santa to visit us by singing 'Jingle Bells' at maximum volume, so of course he duly appeared accompanied by an enormous cheer, and began handing out selection boxes, one for each of us. I decided to save mine for Christmas Day. Gareth broke into his immediately. He'd demolished half of it before it was time to go home. Throughout all of this we all made a constant, cacophonous noise with our chatter and laughter. Some were sick from too much jelly and chocolate and at least one fight would break out somewhere in the room. The annual ritual completed, we would be collected by parents, grandparents, aunties and uncles, who enquired after what we'd asked Santa to bring us for Christmas, and then steered us homeward in the gathering dusk.

The Hoover children's party followed the same general pattern, but there were subtle differences, the most obvious being the sheer scale of the event. In those days, Hoover was one of those paternalistic corporations that believed they had a duty to encourage and support the social lives of their workforce. To that end there were playing fields next to the big factory, and provision for all manner of clubs for enthusiasts to join, encompassing everything from football to amateur radio. The hub of all this activity was the staff club building, just inside the factory gate, and it was here that our children's party was thrown. The high-ceilinged hall where we sat was at least five times the size of the miners' club, and it smelled of floor polish rather than beer. Hundreds of us were packed into the airy space at long tables, and things proceeded in much the same way as they had at the Merthyr Vale Miners' club. The key difference, however, was that in addition to a selection box from Santa, there was a real, substantial present on offer, and a degree of pot luck as to whether you landed a really good one or not. The tension was palpable as, food finished, we again summoned Santa with our singing. It worked this time too, although with the classy additional twist of his arriving on the roof, presumably in his sleigh, and his waving to us through the skylight windows set high above our heads near the ceiling. We were handed little slips of paper to distinguish us as members of one of four groups; older and younger girls, and older and younger boys. Then there was a genuinely agonising wait as we queued to see the man in red himself. We let him know, one by one and solemnly so, what we hoped to receive on Christmas Day and then we were ushered, in line with the slips of paper we clutched tightly, to one of four big screens laid out in the hall, behind which lay four vast mounds of gift wrapped presents. This was genuine Plenty. Almost American in its excess. I was breathless. At random we were handed a gift, and we ran back to our places at the tables to tear off the paper. My parcel was at least three feet long, and when unwrapped a proper fire engine was revealed. It was plastic, so not perfect, but it was vast, and had an extendable ladder. Really something.

I suppose that the Hoover party must have edged it, then, when it came to appealing to the sheer consumerist greed of the under tens. But they never did have proper chips, like the miners did.

Once, in the run up to Christmas, the churches and chapels in the village got together to pay for a large, outdoor Christmas tree. It was erected on the little triangle of public land just next to Mr Rees, the undertaker, right at the end of our street. It was huge. Easily as tall as a house. To complete the wonder of it, coloured electric light bulbs were trailed around its branches. On the night of Christmas Eve we were bundled out into the street wearing bobble hats, duffle coats and mittens, to sing carols around the tree. There was a chant of, 'Three, two, one!' and the power was switched on. The coloured light bulbs sprang into life and stood out like jewels against the dark all around. There was a big crowd gathered about the tree. Churches from all sorts of places must have contributed to the event. There were vicars and priests everywhere, wearing dog collars and shirt fronts of different colours. There was even a monk in a habit, and a Greek Orthodox priest all in black with a stove-pipe hat and several jewel-encrusted crucifixes arranged carefully on his chest. The grown-ups handed out lanterns to us – candles in jam jars fixed with wire to the end of a stick. When we sang 'Silent Night', I looked up at the Christmas tree and its coloured lamps standing out brilliantly against the night sky. I held out my jam jar lantern, its sizzling candle burning away, and I was entirely convinced that no Christmas, anywhere, anytime, could be as wonderful as this.

When Christmas Day itself came, there was no surprise in store, since I had chosen my present months before. In a shop window in Merthyr I had seen a bright yellow Tonka digger. It was huge and made of real metal, not plastic. It had a real hydraulic style digging arm that you worked with your hand at the rear, and a great big shovel up front. Mam had asked the shop to 'put it by' and she had paid for it in instalments, once a week. When I unwrapped it and laid hands on it for the first time, I fell in love with it. It was the very essence of what a toy should be, the distilled, concentrated perfection of toyness. We had stockings too; our football socks stuffed with walnuts and tangerines wrapped in tissue paper. Dad had bought a grossly oversized turkey that barely made it into the oven and that fed us for a week. We passed the holiday watching *Morcambe and Wise* and old movies on the TV whilst Mam cracked walnuts into a bowl, sipping at a drink she called a 'Blue Moon' until she giggled. There was no snow outside but I didn't care. All in all, it was a perfect, happy day.

That winter, my parents took me to a concert. The Ynysowen Male Voice Choir had been recently formed. It was another example of the community organising and gathering together in the wake of the disaster. The core membership of the choir consisted of bereaved fathers. Their concert was to be performed in Capel Aberfan, the biggest chapel in the village. It sat on Aberfan Road, and was much bigger than our own little chapel. It had an upstairs gallery of pews held up with cast iron pillars, but it still had that same unmistakeable chapel smell of furniture polish and the old dry paper of hymn books. We sat downstairs, I remember, and I looked around to see the chapel brightly lit and packed with people, the sheer number of bodies warming the room against the evening chill outside. The choir arranged themselves standing at the front, with a pianist to accompany them. This was to be the first time I ever experienced music performed live; until then I had known only the tinny, transistorised kind.

It was a concert, and they would have sung several hymns and other pieces, but I remember *'Tydi a Roddaist'*. I remember the swelling of their voices and how I felt the sound as much as hearing it, through the soles of my feet and deep in my chest. A plaintive, longing harmony of great power, magnified by the closeness of us all. As they sang I began to understand something. This was more than music that the choir was making, offering. Their rootedness, their strength of will, transmuted into this sound, was being shared with us; all of us. No one in the chapel was in those moments simply a member of an audience, or of a choir. We had become one human heart. One spirit given voice.

What is a 'disaster'? What sets it apart from the griefs experienced by millions, every day, in every country? It is the concentration of loss, in space and in time, the heaping up of sorrow. And when those that are lost are children, well then, you have what Aberfan really means. As the Ynysowen Choir sang that hymn, Aberfan found its voice and I, as young as I was, heard it for the first time. This was a shared outpouring of both the acceptance and defiance of anguish.

Even simply to endure in the face of grief is a courageous thing. But to do more than endure, to sing like this, to make this transfiguring sound, was something beyond courage: it was a redemption of our right to be. I knew then that whatever else happened, Aberfan – this place, these men, all of us – had the *right* to go on. For the first time I felt not just an affection for my home village, but a deep pride in it. At least this one aspect of the indistinct anxieties that had hovered at the edge of my thoughts, and found expression in my dreams, could be laid to rest. I never again dreamed that the pit would swallow us, and I think it was because of that night, because of the choir. I stopped dreaming that the pit would swallow us because this music had taught me that we had a right to be here. These men singing in front of us had purchased that right, over and over. For the first time in my life I was proud of something outside of myself and I realised that I was surrounded by multiple essences of the best that human beings could be. I realised, too, that although grief endures, so does love.

# Walking with my Father

When I was around the age of nine, my father got into the habit of taking me on long weekend walks around the village. The old cinema had by now closed its doors for good and I had more time on my hands. Sometimes Gareth came along and sometimes it was just the two of us, my father and I.

The first step was to gather provisions so we stopped first at the Berni's café where Dad would pick up twenty Players and a bag of Raspberry Ruffles, and I got my two ounces of wine gums in a paper bag. It had to be wine gums for a walk. I'd take a look at the variety of colours so that I could eat them in reverse order of preference, whilst pacing myself carefully so that they would last the whole of the way. Green wine gums would be eaten first, as we set out, since green was my least favourite. I never understood why they bothered making the green ones in the first place; nobody could like them, surely? Then came yellow, then orange, then red, then the most delicious black ones only at the end, when we were nearly home again.

Our route generally took us southwards along the old canal bank, and we walked it many times, in all the seasons of the year. We'd join the pathway part way up the hill leading to the cemetery, just where the old Aberfan railway station had once been. This railway track had been long since abandoned, leaving only one line, on the Merthyr Vale side of the valley. The old track bed was still walkable in places though, and ran by constraint of topology pretty much parallel to the route of the old canal. We would pass the three-storey backs of Bryn Taff on our right, then Kingsley Terrace, then Pleasant View. Then we reached the old lock house, still there, though marooned for good now and bereft of its old purpose since the canal had silted up years before and the last barge had long since made its way to Cardiff, never to return. Passing the lock house meant that we were now entering the nearest thing to proper countryside our valley could boast. Here we left the village behind. The cliffs of the Darren were on our right, and could be seen through the foliage of enormous beech trees rooted amongst a tumble of boulders, some of them as big as houses. These were the result of another, natural, landslide, one that had happened long before our village had ever existed, back when our valley was ancient woodland, and the River Taff had salmon in it, leaping their way back to their spawning grounds. There was a line of electricity pylons here, running along the face of the cliff, roped together like mountaineers. It was rumoured that halfway up the cliff face was a small cave called 'Cromwell's Cave'. This was because it had been used as a hiding place by royalist fugitives who were fleeing Cromwell's New Model Army. Or by Roundheads who were fleeing vengeful Cavaliers. It depended on who was telling the story.

We might spend some time exploring amongst the beech trees. Dad showed me that their strange three-sided nuts were edible, though it seemed hardly worth it as they were so small and bitter. In spring the ground here was awash with a haze of bluebells, and we might have been a thousand miles away from any industry, despite the clanking of coal wagons that could still be faintly heard just up the valley. On one occasion I came across the biggest and highest and best rope swing I had ever encountered. It was tied high in the branches of one of the beech trees, and I straight away pestered my father so that I could try it out. He was reluctant but eventually relented. I swung out, full of bravado, despite the fact that the ground fell away alarmingly because of the steepness of the slope. I must have been at least twenty feet above the ground when I fell. I landed flat on my back, on the leaf mould covered ground, with a tremendous thud. I remember lying there and looking directly upward at the dappled sunlight between the topmost leaves, and feeling awfully relieved since I didn't seem to be hurting at all. Then, when I tried to breathe in, I found I couldn't. Having the wind knocked out of me was a new experience and I panicked until my father scrambled down the slope to reach me and hauled me up onto my feet. I was white with shock, he told me later, and trembling. Slowly, very slowly, my ability to take a breath began to return. Little coloured lights seemed to dance in the fluid of my eyeballs.

'Best not mention that to your mother,' Dad said.

Further along the path were smaller trees: hazel, hawthorn and some willow, and the landscape opened up a little so that we could see across to Merthyr Vale on the other side of the valley. Here in springtime I'd collect sprigs of pussy willow and may blossom to take home for Mam, and later in the year I stuffed my pockets with hazelnuts, although I always seemed to pick them when they weren't quite ripe. Dad told me that you could eat the leaves of the hawthorn trees, and that they were called 'poor man's bread and cheese', and he chomped on a few by way of demonstration. I thought they tasted foul.

Once, we cut ourselves an arrow-straight willow rod with Dad's penknife, and we sat on the tussocky grass while he showed me how to peel off a strip of bark scored with the knife in a double spiral down the length of it, to make a decorated walking stick. I held onto that walking stick for many years but it's lost now.

At Pontygwaith, we left the canal bank and headed downhill for the old humpback bridge across the river, almost completely hidden by trees as it spanned the Taff running between steep-sided banks. Here I would run ahead to find some small stones to line up on the parapet of the bridge, and flick them off one by one for them to plop into the river below. For the simple joy of it.

Our route now took us uphill again, this time on the Merthyr Vale side of the river. There was an old abandoned World War Two pillbox here, though heaven knows why – there seemed to be nothing worth defending down this way. I always nipped inside to look around, but there was nothing there but rotting leaves on the floor and the smell of damp concrete. Then, on a little way to join the pathway that would lead us back home. This particular trackway had a special history. Cut into the hillside, the ground falling away steeply below it, it was by now overshadowed by large beech trees and in parts it was overgrown, but it was still possible to see, here and there, large stone blocks protruding from the earth. Each block had indentations carved into it, all identical. These blocks were railway sleepers, and it was here, in 1804, that the first ever steam locomotive in the world had run on rails. Designed by the Cornish engineer, Richard Trevithick, the event was prompted by a bet between two ironmasters, and the engine hauled wagons holding a load of iron and men the ten miles or so between Penydarren and Abercynon – the world's first railway journey.

My father told me the story every time we passed this way, and I was happy to listen whilst I searched for more of the sleeper stones by kicking away their covering layer of moss and grass, as the modern railway running on a trackbed a little further up the hill clattered above us. He told the story with a mixture of pride and aggravation. Pride because our valley had been first, and aggravation because all the credit for the first railway journey had gone to Stephenson and his 'Rocket' which had run on the Liverpool-Manchester railway some twenty-five years later. It was not the last time, by any means, that I would hear a story of how the Valleys had been overlooked, and our achievements sidelined or forgotten.

It was time to strike out for home now, along to the Black Lion signal box and to Merthyr Vale. Time to contemplate the red and black wine gums still in my pocket.

My father and I must have walked that route dozens of times and I cherished the time I spent with him. Sometimes we talked incessantly all the way, sometimes in companionable silence, always happily. My Dad, despite, or perhaps because of, his upbringing in this most industrial of places, was always drawn to the countryside. In the summer holidays he would drag us along to agricultural shows in Brecon or Abergavenny, which I must admit bored me, but he would stand for hours admiring the animals and had a special fondness for horses. It was as if he felt he had missed out on something. He bought me Spotter's books to identify birds, animal paw prints and the different kinds of trees, and I would devour them, reading them over and over and ticking off those I had seen; the paw prints were always in short supply.

On one of these walks, as spring was giving way to summer, while I was clambering amongst the boulders at the foot of the Darren, quite suddenly and seemingly on a whim, my Dad said, 'Come on, Huwcyn, let's go all the way to the top.' And gestured up towards the mountain. I was thrilled. I had never been to the top of the mountain before. When I was very young I had looked up to the row of trees that stood along the topmost ridge, silhouetted against the skyline. They could be seen clearly from the vantage point of our front doorstep in Cottrell Street. I had always thought them to be an impossibly long way off. I had convinced myself that since they were so distant and yet so prominent they must have great significance, and I had decided that they must mark the border with England.

So we set off uphill, skirting the cliff face of the Darren and following a meandering sheep track through heather and ground-hugging wimberry bushes. The going was steep and our progress was slow since we had to navigate between dense patches of bracken too thick to walk through. As I kicked along, I disturbed large grasshoppers that bounced off my bare knees, their touch dry and papery. I caught one in the cupped palms of my hand, and when I opened my fingers to take a closer look it kicked itself away into the air. We stopped on the edge of what must have once been a small quarry, carved into the hillside, its edges now smoothed over by the growth of heather. We sat for a breather on the lip of the quarry and took in the view. I had never been so high up above the village. It was as if we had taken up our seats in an opera box, looking down at the place I knew so well but rendered strange from this great height, all laid out like a stage-set far below. I saw the village, the pit, and the river with new eyes as they were reduced to toy-like dimensions by the distance. I realised how confined and cramped my view of things had been until now. It was exhilarating. I popped a wine gum in my mouth by way of celebration, and Dad smoked a cigarette.

'It'll keep the midges off us,' he said, puffing away. Although I never saw any.

I looked behind me up to the mountain top – there was still a long way to go. And so we laboured on, the muscles in my legs beginning to protest as we climbed towards the summit. Then suddenly, the ground simply flattened out, and we were standing on flat moorland. I felt a little deflated. I had anticipated a jagged, pointy mountain summit, just like the one in photographs I'd seen of Hilary and Tensing on the top of Everest. My father explained to me that this mountain, like all the mountains separating the communities of the Valleys was flat topped; in fact this moorland was the original ground level of this part of Wales until Ice Age glaciers had come and gouged out the Valleys themselves. We were standing on original earth, the valley simply a scar carved out of it. The trees I knew from peering up at them from the valley floor, the trees that stood silhouetted against the skyline, were on the mountain top to our left, and we were definitely not in England. Just walk a little further that way, explained my father, and another valley, the Cynon Valley would open up, and then another mountain, and then the Rhondda Valley, then another and another, all the way to the Amman Valley, on the western edge of the coalfield where they still spoke Welsh. England was in fact in completely the opposite direction, and a long way off.

We walked along the mountain top and the ground was peppered with thick clumps of coarse, wild grass and domed anthills with wimberry and heather in between. There was sunshine, and a gentle breeze blowing, and I began to feel happier with my lot. We had left behind the confines of the valley and suddenly the sky had doubled in size. The last time I had experienced openness like this had been on the sands at low tide on Barry Island. My world had expanded hugely, my perspective permanently altered. The sound of the colliery and the railway had been swallowed by the valley sides, and up here there was just the sound of the wind whispering through the grass and the occasional baa-ing of a distant sheep.

Then there was a faint trilling of a bird, far off, and barely audible.

'Skylarks,' said Dad. 'Come on, I'll show you how to listen for them, and you see if you can spot one. It's hard to see them, because they're so small and fly so high.' Then he lay flat on his back on the grass to look directly upwards at the sky, and gestured for me to do the same alongside him.

'They're high up,' he said, 'really high. And they're really small too. Listen to them singing, and look carefully.'

With my head on the ground and sheltered from the wind, the ethereal sound of the skylark's song magnified in volume. A tumbling of high notes. It was beautiful. I strained my eyes to see the birds, and fancied that far, far above us a tiny speck of life was swooping through the sky. I did not want to spoil the sound with speaking so I simply pointed at the speck, and my father nodded. I looked directly upward again, so that the whole of my field of vision was the blue of the sky, and the white of small clouds. And the skylarks sang. I felt a deep peace, and imagined the world turning beneath me.

Then it happened. For the second and last time. For a brief moment, just a moment, my perception shifted, as it had that once before when I lay on the coal shed roof in my grandfather's garden. It was as if the coverings of the world had slipped away, and there was no barrier between my thoughts and the world around. There was the sky, and the birdsong, and the earth and me; and then quite suddenly we were all one and the same.

Now, as I recall those two moments and struggle to translate into words clear enough to transmit to others, to myself, how this felt, I find I cannot. Not completely. It was not simply a 'feeling', it was more a 'knowing'. I knew, beyond all doubt, that if I, the sky, the earth and the skylark's song were suddenly all to disappear, everything would still *be*. That besides our size and shape and weight and appearance there was something else, something far more important and substantial behind all that: the underlying stuff of the universe. The thing that held all the other things together.

Maybe this sounds a little crazy. Maybe those two occasions, both involving a change in perception through filling my vision with a peaceful sky, and also the feeling of unshakeable security and happiness that those two moments had in common, simply threw some kind of switch inside my brain and I, for a few seconds, went into some kind of trance. I don't know. Maybe.

What is definitely true is that I have never forgotten those two instances in time. I can recall them with a vivid clarity in a way that I can recall no other memories, not even the most happy, most sad or most visceral. They stand apart, and I have thought about them often throughout my life.

And this is what I learned: there is a depth to our existence on this earth that we cannot, as a rule, see or feel. You might call it spirit, or talk about the presence of the sacred, or take it as a prompt to pray to God. It does not matter. I mean, the language does not matter. If you set out to describe it, words will not get you even halfway there. If you set out to describe it, you will fail.

The moment passed, but the sense of peace and happiness remained, and while we still lay on the ground alongside each other, staring into blueness, I reached out and held my father's hand, and the skylark's song filled the sky. If I were to conjure the sound of perfect happiness, it would be the song of that little bird. I said nothing about my momentary episode of feeling beyond the world and of the world at the same instant, in fact neither I nor my father said anything at all. There were no words, just the blue of the sky, the weight of my body on the earth and the birdsong.

As the years have passed, the significance of that day, the day I walked along the mountain top with my father, has only become magnified for me. It is my fondest memory of him. He had shown me the wideness of the world and just how beautiful it could be. He had shown me how to properly listen to a skylark's song. And almost certainly without knowing it, he had shown me peace of mind.

Many years later, when I was in my forties, and had been representing my home community as a full time politician for some while, my father succumbed to cancer.

Not long before he died I fought an election campaign. We hired the old library in Aberfan as a venue to stuff envelopes with my election address, and party members came from all over the constituency to volunteer their help. I had been out canvassing door-to-door and joined them part-way through the job. I went about the trestle tables saying hello to everyone and thanking them for their help. Someone said hello. He was old and frail and wore a cap pulled down as to be almost covering his eyes. I did not recognise him. I said hello in return. It was only after the word had left my lips that I saw it was my father.

In the two or three days since I had last seen him, his face had so changed, become so gaunt, that for a moment, and with that cap, I had not known him. When I realised, the moment swallowed me whole. The wretchedness of it.

As I saw him so ill, that day and the days that followed, I tried to picture him instead as he was on that day on the mountain: young, composed and happy. I still do.

One day, during his months of illness, I picked up on the radio while I was driving a performance of Vaughan Williams' 'The Lark Ascending'. The connection with the memory of that day lodged itself in my mind, and I will always, now, associate that piece of music with my father. I don't know what he'd make of that; he was a fan more of Louis Armstrong at the one extreme and Puccini at the other, his work sung, preferably, by the Swedish tenor, Jussi Bjorling.

It was only in the writing of this book that I looked into what had inspired Ralph Vaughan Williams to write the piece. It turned out to be a poem of the same name, by George Meredith (1828-1909), an extract of which is here:

## The Lark Ascending

*He rises and begins to round,*
*He drops the silver chain of sound*
*Of many links without a break,*
*In chirrup, whistle, slur and shake*
*All intervolved and spreading wide,*
*Like water dimples down a tide*
*Where ripple ripple overcurls*

*And eddy into eddy whirls;*
*A press of hurried notes that run*
*So fleet they scarce are more than one...*

*... And you shall hear the herb and tree,*
*the better heart of men shall see,*
*shall feel celestially, as long*
*As you crave nothing save the song.*

*...For singing till his heaven fills,*
*'Tis love of earth that he instils,*
*And ever winging up and up,*
*Our valley is his golden cup,*
*And he the wine that overflows*
*To lift us with him as he goes...*

All very Victorian pastoral and, I think, quite, quite wonderful. Here in these lines is the closest rendering I am ever likely to see of what I heard and felt on that day for I did, certainly, get the chance to 'feel celestially' and I saw the possibility of purity in human experience, as well as the reality of our connectedness. The native Americans say that all things are connected. I had felt the connection of sky to earth, and of myself to both; the 'silver chain of sound' binding us together and making all this perceptible.

Last year I took my own two sons, James and Sam, along that same route which my father and I had walked that day. I think I wanted to show them a place which might still bear an imprint of an old happiness. We walked along the old Glamorganshire canal bank, now known as the Taff Trail. It has a tarmac surface now, and the A470 dual carriageway runs alongside it. Traffic roars over the spot where the old Lock House once stood. We climbed the mountain by the same route my father and I had taken more than forty years before. We made our way uphill through the beech wood. It was too late in the year for bluebells, but there was still a rope swing hanging from one of the great beech trees. James tried it out. He didn't fall.

When we got as far as the little disused quarry, we stopped for our lunch. I'd filled a rucksack at the Co-op with sandwiches and pork pies and bottles of water. I'd slipped in a bag of wine gums, too, just in case. I told my sons about the school holiday, some time after my father had shown me this place, when I had come here with a group of friends, and we had built a den. It took us several days, but it was worth it. It had dry-stone walls and a turf roof. We built a hearth inside and lit a fire. The roof kept out most of the rain, and the fire drew a treat through a hole in it, but our attempts at cooking were a mess. When our baked potatoes came out incinerated and black, we melted fruit pastilles on the hot stones instead. When my friends and I had sat on the lip of the quarry we had looked down on the whole village as if we were kings of the mountain. We stayed there all day, for days on end, until each evening hunger drove us home for our tea.

James and Sam began firing questions at me, about the den, about my childhood, about how old I had been when this had happened (about ten, I think). For a brief moment I thought I'd finally managed to impress my own children with a story from my past. It turned out, though, that what had impressed them was not the effort in building such an ambitious den, half way up a mountainside, or even the childhood fire-lighting. It was the freedom. The freedom my generation had to wander as far from home as we liked, or at least as far as we could manage; to stay out all day long without adult supervision, to simply mess about in the open air with no plans, no club that need be joined, no organisation or any particular aim and no obligation to report home until darkness fell. They thought it anarchic. And so it was.

My sons and I struck out uphill again and eventually the ground levelled out and there we were on the mountain top. We took a 'selfie' on the way. It was the wrong time of year for skylarks to be singing. We took in the view and I bored the boys with talk about glaciers.

As we began to descend the mountain there was a sudden, torrential cloudburst. I struggled to help Sam put on his waterproof over-trousers, and I panicked slightly, because he was shivering with cold and already wet through.

Perhaps this had been a mistake, I thought, he was still so young, and perhaps this walk was too much for him. He saw the worry in my face, and I felt a little pang of shame. I was flapping and panicking in front of my little boy. I was worrying him when he should be confident and happy. So I calmed myself, trying to reassure. But to myself I thought: perhaps I'm not the father my father was, just as this place is not quite the place it was. I had never seen my father act like this. He always seemed calm and self-assured, always knowing just what to say and do, at least while I was very young. The very idea of packing waterproof trousers for a simple walk on the mountain would have struck him as amusing.

A wave of mournfulness swept over me and I saw: we cannot have it back, any of it. We might see it in a dream, or linger on a memory of it, but the thing itself is gone. Gone utterly. I wondered then if there were any real point in this, in dragging my sons on a tour of the ruins of my childhood, the ruins of old love; my love for this place, my love for my father, now made one-sided by death. I could not ever recreate that day my father had made for me, no matter how hard I tried, or how often, because I was not him.

What had his thoughts been, I wondered, as he looked at his son, playing on this mountain top more than forty years ago? Had he been reliving old memories that day too? It was obvious he had been this way before, after all.

But he had not spoken of his memories when we had passed this way together. He had simply shown me the view beyond the valley and how best to listen to the singing of the larks. And so I made a memory of my very own, fresh that day.

The thing itself is gone. But it will be remade. Always a little different, but containing within itself the same truth. The truth now seen through our children's eyes.

But for me – for myself alone – if I could relive just one day of all the days of my childhood, it would be that day. The day my father showed me the breadth of the earth, the immensity of the sky, and how best to hear the skylark's song.

# Epilogue

After the disaster, each individual, each family in the village, had their own path to tread, their own inheritance from that day in October 1966. For some there was raw heartbreak; for some anxiety; for some depression; for some all of these things. But so far as it is possible for a community as a whole to respond with compassion and courage to such a blow, then Aberfan and Merthyr Vale did so. Despite all the horror of that October day, I can testify that the village was a warm and wonderful place in which to grow up.

Twenty years on from the disaster, the sibling villages had another blow to bear, however. Something that would change forever the very manner of place that they were.

Like the rest of the South Wales coalfield, the collective trauma of the miners' strike of 1984-5 showed these strong, decent communities at their very best, and I saw the truest nature of their obstreperous, mighty heart.

But the strike was lost, of course. The miners marched back to work behind their lodge banner, and Merthyr Vale Colliery finally closed in 1989. Suddenly, Aberfan was no longer a pit village. The original, first cause for there being a village called

Aberfan at all had ceased to be. In retrospect I see that I had been of the final generation to grow up with the lived experience of the South Wales coalfield all about me. Its life lived day to day, through which values like solidarity and sacrifice were not mere words but vivid reality, had its last great outpouring before I had reached my twenty-first birthday.

The social and economic consequences of losing the strike, for the whole of the coalfield, were calamitous. The communities of the Valleys, Aberfan included, are still living with the effects.

My experiences during the strike (I was a student at the time) woke a political passion within me that was to last a lifetime. Surely, I thought, if the raw power of government can do such harm to people and communities, such long-lasting damage, then it can only be a duty to fight to capture that power and use it instead to protect places like the South Wales Valleys. And even though the pits were by then soon to disappear, the better values of the people that had lived about them, their humane and singular culture, still bore lessons for the future – for the kind of people we were set to become.

I was elected to the Welsh Assembly in 1999 to represent Merthyr Tydfil & Rhymney, the constituency which includes my home village. I was to spend seventeen years as an Assembly Member, and at the forefront of my mind throughout all that time was the still desperate need to mitigate the effects of that sudden collapse of the local economy brought about by the pit closure programme of the 1980s. More than that, I felt that there were values still, that Aberfan had taught me, that informed the choices to be made about the future, about the paths still to be chosen.

As part of my work in the Assembly I lobbied the then First Minister, Rhodri Morgan, for the return of the money taken from the people of Aberfan to pay for the clean-up operation of the Pantglas tip in the 1960s. Rhodri and his government, to their eternal credit, readily agreed. I insisted the sum allocated should be adjusted for inflation and any lost interest; I reckoned the sum to be around £2 million. In 2007, the Welsh Government paid £1.5 million into the Aberfan Memorial Charity and a further £0.5 million into the Aberfan Educational Charity. I was glad to see it done, but it was not something to celebrate. It should never have been necessary.

Aberfan today is a quieter, greener place than it has been for any time since the 1860s. The old colliery site is grassed over and is awaiting a new housing development. The River Taff runs clear and clean; you can fish for trout there and otters and kingfishers live along its banks. The tips are gone.

Aberfan, and its people, remain.

# Acknowledgements

My thanks go to the writer and teacher of writers, Tessa Hadley. Without Tessa's willingness to give her time to reading an early draft of this memoir and offering her indispensable advice, it would simply never have been completed.

I am grateful, also, to my editor Professor Dai Smith, for his encouragement and infectious enthusiasm and to Richard Davies and Alison Evans at Parthian Books for their patience and support.

My gratitude to David Davies, a friend and a survivor of Pantglas Junior School, encompasses not only his willingness to offer comment on my manuscript, but also his years of selfless service to the people of Aberfan through his work with the Aberfan Memorial Charity.

I am grateful to the Rev. June Vaughan and the congregation of Zion Methodist Chapel, Aberfan, for the chance to reproduce the cover picture, and for all that went before.

The staff of Merthyr Central Library and of Aberfan Library have been unfailingly generous with their time in helping me with this work, as was Geoff Matsell at the 'Old Merthyr Tydfil' website.

Thanks are owed to my family; to my mother for sharing her memories and for her love for all of us. To my sister Anne for her forthright (and wholly deserved) comments on my style of writing and to my brother Gareth who grew up alongside me in the aftermath of 1966. My wife Lynne and my sons, James and Sam, deserve a thank you for putting up with my prolonged absences whilst I was writing this book.

Finally, a particular thank you goes to my sister, Allyson, for her courage and for her defiance of the dark.

# Modern Wales

In 2017 Parthian Books, supported by the Rhys Davies Trust and edited by Dai Smith, launched a new series entitled Modern Wales. The series intends to look at places crucial to the development of modern Wales, such as Cardiff and Newport, as well as at the imagery and iconography which has shaped the culture and society of modern Wales. The series, in a new and distinctive livery, will include an impressive back catalogue of connected Parthian publications. The inaugural titles of the series are *To Hear the Skylark's Song* by Huw Lewis, and *Merthyr: The Crucible of Modern Wales* by Joe England. Future titles, already commissioned will include Angela John's *Rocking the Boat*, essays on Welsh women who pioneered the fight for equality, and Daryl Leeworthy's, *Labour Country*, a fresh and provocative look at the struggle through radical action for social democracy in Wales. In the pipeline already are new political and culturally-informed biographies of the pioneering socialist and feminist Minnie Pallister by Alun Burge and of the great Welsh novelist, playwright and public commentator, Gwyn Thomas.

*the* Rhys Davies Trust

Huw (standing) and Gareth. Summer 1966,
Cottrell Street, Aberfan.

The coal waste tips above Pantglas,
Aberfan a few days after the disaster
*Courtesy of Alan George's Old Merthyr Tydfil*
*(www.alangeorge.co.uk)*

The landslide and the village, taken from a point above the tip. Pantglas Junior school is shown partially buried in the centre-right of the photo.
*Courtesy of Alan George's Old Merthyr Tydfil*
*(www.alangeorge.co.uk)*

Volunteer rescue workers at Pantglas Junior School.
The right-hand side, and much of the rear of
the school has been destroyed.
*Courtesy of Alan George's Old Merthyr Tydfil*
*(www.alangeorge.co.uk)*

Rescue workers moving wood and other obstacles.
(Huw's father can be seen in profile in the centre).
*Courtesy of Mirrorpix*

Residents and rescue workers dig for survivors amid the wreckage of Aberfan's primary school, 21 October 1966
*Courtesy of Getty Images*

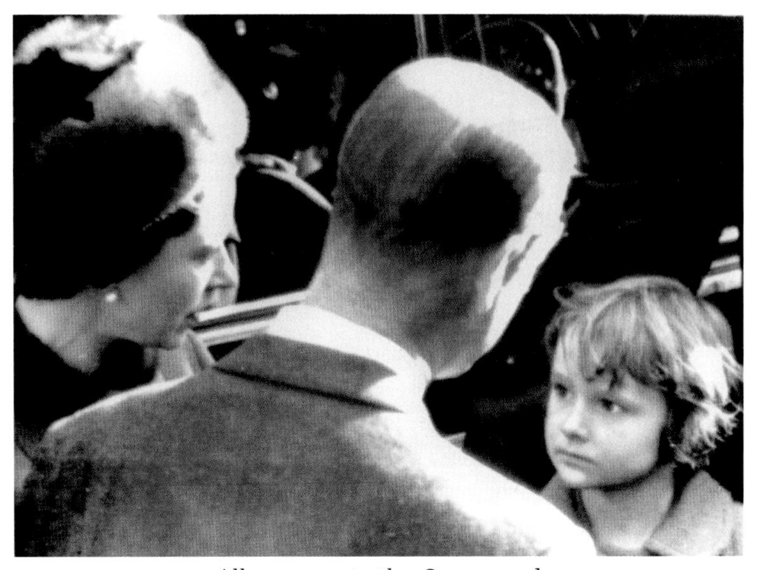

Allyson meets the Queen and
Duke of Edinburgh days after the disaster.
*Courtesy of Merthyr Public Library*

NCB Coal train steaming towards Merthyr Vale Colliery
*Courtesy of Alan George's Old Merthyr Tydfil*
*(www.alangeorge.co.uk)*